Pearl

Pearl

THE ART OF BEING FOUND, LOVED, AND VALUED IN THE HEART OF GOD

ROXANNA GRIMES

TATE PUBLISHING
AND **ENTERPRISES, LLC**

Acknowledgments

I want to thank the Original Pearl
Girl Workshop participants:
Elyse, Tess, Jordyn, Jaydah, Jaylee,
Jaclyn, Camille, Erin, Rachel
You are the Pearl Girl Home Group. Loved. Always. Period.

The Original Pearl Girl Workshop would not have happened
without the love and dedication of Squad
and Pearl coaches! I love you!
Gaby, Sydney, Becky, Kim N., Kim A., Tami

The two pilot pearl study groups from
Shoreline Baptist Church:
Janae, Arin, Carlee, Kato, Katelynn,
Zaida, Betty, Sheila, April

Stephanie Tucker, my dear friend and teacher,

thank you for pouring out to me and so many others.
The pouring out led to the conception of *Pearl*.
(Stephanie is the author of *The Christian Codependence
Workbook* and *The House that Grace Built*.)

The beautiful jewelry and scarves made
by Christie and Shaila for Pearl.
My dear friend Patty, author of *The Peace House* series.
So grateful for her feather counting and prayers.
My dear friend Taprina, who never gave up on my writing.
Thank you, Darla, for your assistance in the manuscript.

My tenderhearted husband, Guy, for all your
patience, love, service, and belief in *Pearl*.
I love you.

My great son, Greyson, thank you for carrying
the message before I even understood it.
I love you.

Uncle Bobby and Aunt Dian (adopted me), thank you
for being my mom and dad and telling me in more ways
than words can say that I am meant to be. I love you.

For the girls whose stories are told in these
pages. In your honor, I changed your names.
Thank you for the sacred privilege of walking beside you.

My heart is overflowing with a good theme.
I recite my composition concerning my King.

—Psalm 45:1

Contents

our children in sports and educational systems designed to make everyone a winner. Everyone received a trophy at the end of the day. We raised children in a system of lies. The main lie being, "I am *entitled*." But everyone knows that every person can't win all the time.

More importantly, out of the self-esteem movement, my generation raised children in another worldview. This worldview has served to deeply wound girls in our culture, especially Christian girls. That worldview is feminism, and *feminism* has served to strip them of knowing God's true design. Feminism seeks to make all things *equal*. God's design is higher than man's ways, though, and seeks to reveal everyone's *value*.

Feminism: "The belief in the need to secure rights and opportunities for women equal to those of men, or a commitment to securing these."1 The key word: equal. Since when did *equal* offer real and lasting value? Yes, it's true, we are all made in God's image, but to make equal the reference point for value is so limiting when we are fashioned and designed from the heart of God and by His highly fashionable hand.

We are in the fourth generation of women who have chased after and demanded equal rights, when in fact the real longing is to feel whole and valued. While we are busy pursuing equality, claiming our worldly titles and entitles, we raise girls who, as a consequence, lose their childhood girlhood, femininity, and purity. One of the most devastating

---

1   Encarta dictionary

effects of this movement on culture has been abortion, sexual promiscuity, and divorce.

I know families who have more aborted babies in heaven than they have on earth (and no one was poor or raped). I know people who died as a direct or indirect link to divorce and its devastation. Yet we fight to save the spotted owl, whales, and various butterflies, not to mention a rather large collection of other environmental causes. I know Christian girls raised in godly homes who have found themselves swimming in a sexual sea of desire and addictive patterns. I hear their confessions in my office.

Why do we divorce, abort, and play with sex? I believe it's because we bought into the lie that we have the right to be happy, pleasured, comfortable, and free to search for more happiness, comfort, and freedom. We believe that we are entitled to find our true happiness. The lie goes even deeper for some who believe this Christian worldview: God loves me and wants me to be happy.

Sadly, though, no one appears to be happy. When a mother is unhappy and still engaged in an elusive pursuit of her *entitled* happiness, she often abandons her daughter to spend countless hours in a career while sending her daughter off to be safely supervised by someone else. There is more concern about so-called "safe" babysitters than there is about the inner workings of a growing girl's heart. Abandoned women abandon others. Abortion, divorce, cohabitating, and sexual promiscuity teach daughters that it's all about us. We have a right to be happy, and so they will just have to figure out how to be happy too. And it does just the opposite. These things actually cause value and happiness to leak out.

Many girls aren't happy. They are despairing, and always seeking the twinkle, the spark, the something her heart craves. Twelve-year-olds and younger are *sexting*, and twentysomethings are engaged in live pornography and cybersex. An enormous amount of girls engaged in lesbian culture not only demonstrate adult activity while in an intermediate stage of development, but also *twisted* adult activity while in an intermediate developmental stage!

Today's girlhood and womanhood, and consequently daughterhood and motherhood, is like that of an undeveloped pearl lost in the deep sea floating without direction in search of being known, loved, and secured. It is a sea of inner emotional bondage and physical cravings that can never get enough, whether it's sex, image, validation, attention, love, food, pills, needles, or alcohol. "Wait a minute," you say. "Aren't you speaking to Christian girls?" This is what I see in the counseling rooms concerning Christian girls, and certainly in those who aren't. There isn't a distinction anymore. But Father God wants to identify those girls who choose to move from being a floating and unknown tomb to becoming a God-appointed womb like the oyster host is for a developing pearl. Father longs for them to accept the life He wants to breathe into them. He wants to ransom lost pearls and bring them forth in true beauty and value.

Without God it's a dead end. A tomb. But He is not surprised by any of this. After all, He passed through a tomb to breathe life into yours.

So here we are with our daughters, granddaughters, and nieces in their teens, twenties, and thirties searching for connection and purpose. They only have a diet of quick fixes and being accidently led into carrying our afflictions, resentments, and unforgiveness on their back…and in their soul. I say *accidently* because it isn't conscious on our part. It is no accident, however, on the part of Satan. If he can take down the original design and purpose of womanhood, he takes out the heart of a family, and the culture follows. His design is for us to be mighty in God, nurturing, guiding, content, and easily entreated.

Womanhood is in a cultural fight to figure out how to feel something real and good instead of feeling so dead and empty that they hurt themselves to simply feel something. And before the enemy whispers to you that this is a blame game, simple cause and effect, listen to God's whispers instead: "My daughters, you are valuable and worthwhile. You can't make your value happen. I already did. I had the idea of you and I liked it. So I put you in your momma's womb at just the right moment. Like the parasite that makes its way into the oyster host, I knew you would have difficulties, but I have been with you and never left you. I am passionate about your presence and your purpose. Find your true value in my love and presence. This is couture of the highest cost."

Being valuable doesn't come in a feeling. It comes in a person. And that is what this little book is all about. Father decides we are valuable, chases after us to teach us this, fights battles over and around us every day, and wins the war for us. He is very real and present. He longs to plant His message of value upon your heart toward yourself and your daughter(s). You are His daughter, a treasured pearl to be brought forth from His best fashion and design collection. Ladies, let's reclaim the culture in His name. The definition of couture is *high-fashion designing*. Perhaps girl culture and its endless search for value can take on its true name: Pearl Couture. Girls and women embracing value and identity fashioned and designed by the Most High God.

It has been a painful process as Father has formed this message in my heart. But it is worth it. I am worth it and so are you. God is putting his handprint all over us—especially through the betrayals of others and against ourselves. Every time His hand moved in me, a pearl was left in its place. Will you let Him pearl you?

Introduction

Parasite to Pearl

EVERY GIRL HAS longings. Most girls carry pain. It doesn't matter where she comes from. If you are a girl, you long for something. Longings are what your heart stretches out to find. But until it's found, the heart still longs, even aches, to be known.

Some girls ache with disappointment and long to fill the hole with *anything*. Other girls feel rejection when they are alone, and so they make sure they are never alone. Other girls experience hurt so deep that when they see something they want, they will do *anything* to get it. The cycles repeat.

Unmet longings and unspoken pain drive girls to people, places, and things instead of the One who can satisfy all her needs. Knowing her true identity and personal value remains indefinable as long as she temporarily quenches the thirst with *anything* and *anyone*. Yet while she searches frantically, Jesus Christ has this one longing: to satisfy her.

Like a pearl forming in the hidden recesses of an oyster, she is a pearl in the heart of God. He longs to reveal to her His delight in her and the great price He paid to unveil her precious worth, and to satisfy her. "The Kingdom of heaven is like treasure hidden in a field, which a man found and covered up. Then in his joy he goes and sells all that he has and buys that field." The parable of the Pearl of Great Value continues in verses 45–46. "Again, the kingdom of heaven is like a merchant in search of fine pearls, who, on finding one pearl of great value, went and sold all that he had and bought it" (Matt. 13:44–46, AMP).

This book is written to help girls discover their own God-given identity and the value it places on them. Every girl has a man-made identity of some kind, but it changes with every crowd they hang with. For some girls, longings grow to such an ache that by the time I meet them in the counseling room they have had multiple abortions, multiple sexual partners, drug overdoses, STDs, and hate their parents. And many were raised in a church pew every Sunday. Every time it turns out to be a core issue of identity and value.

If you are a girl aching for anything or anyone to fill the holes in your heart, God wants you to know this:

> He had the idea of you, and He liked it so much that He planted you in your momma's womb while knowing the difficulties you would face in this life.

But He has lovingly brought you through to tell you He is passionate about your presence and purpose in the world. You are a pearl of great worth. Always. Period.

"For you did form my inward parts; You did knit me together in my mother's womb. I will confess and praise You for You are fearful and wonderful and for the awful wonder of my birth! Wonderful are Your works, and that my inner self knows right well. My frame was not hidden from You when I was being formed in secret and intricately and curiously wrought in the depths of the earth. Your eyes saw my unformed substance, and in Your book all the days of my life were written before ever they took shape, when as yet there was none of them" Psalm 139:13–17.

It doesn't matter where you have been or what has happened so far in your life. You are already deeply loved in your present stage of life—way beyond any love known between humans. It's never too late for the One who made you to change the ending to your story. It starts here. Please consider coming to know the One who made you. You will find inner peace, identity, and value not made with human hands, but by God's. He is the only source of true and lasting satisfaction in your longings to be loved, secure, and known.

This love is not dutiful. He actually delights in who He designed—you. But like the parasite that enters the oyster shell to eventually become a beautiful pearl—you, in your lovely design, are created with a God-given need to be unconditionally loved and known. This need expresses itself like a parasite, feeding off anything and everything until it is filled and satisfied. The purpose of this God-given need is to drive you to the love and security of your Creator where you find out who you are and what your purpose is. Just like the pearl that takes eight to twenty years to form, your journey as a girl is intended to birth your true identity and worth. But if you ignore this intended purpose, the parasites will continue eating you on the inside and your identity will remain lost in the journey of survival.

In addition to the pain of unmet love needs, other parasites may enter our personal development. It might be sexual abuse, missing parents, addiction, relentless guilt, and continuously misplaced affections. Some come by way of another person, and some by our own choices. Regardless of the source, the parasites have an intended purpose and are there in the hope a pearl will form. Will you let them have purpose?

As you read this, if you find yourself at the bottom of an ocean-like pit, please know there is still love, companionship, and purpose waiting for you from the One who actually had the original idea of you. God's love and purpose reaches much deeper than the haunting longings at the bottom of your personal pit. He will meet you right where you are. For some girls, their pit is rooted in insecurity and results in abusive cycles with relationship to self-injury, parents, boyfriends, sexual addiction, substance, or school bullies. Maybe your pit is that you hate what you see when you look in the mirror. But this is not what defines you. Your identity is not found in your issues. It can only be found in the One who lifts you from the pit of issues.

My prayer for you is that this work can hopefully drive you to the healing love of God. As you progress through the pages of *Pearl*, we will work backward through the Principles and Biblical Truths in Pearl Couture (on page 193–195) because everything begins with love. Love is the key that unlocks the door to value.

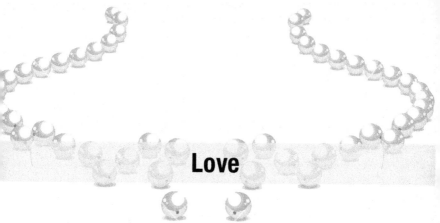

Love

Biblical Truth

> He shall cover you with His feathers, and
> under His wings you shall take refuge; His
> truth shall be your shield and buckler.
>
> —Psalm 91:1–6

Value Concept

GOD'S LOVE IS Home. It is a divinely appointed inward space
I share with Him where I am found, valued, and secured to
the core.

Battle Cry

I will be found, held together, and grown up in the love of
Jesus Christ.

Application

God's love is my home. This love is the place I return to many times in a moment to find my worth and the desire to live it out.

Pearl of Great Worth

REGARDLESS OF YOUR current pit status, the only remedy for getting out is through His love. An authentic encounter with His love will completely change your view of everything, starting with you. Being the One who made you and treasures you, God's able to expose and destroy lies that are set up against that truth. This is done through a personal revelation of His love. Like myself, most of the girls and young women in my office come to discover they have had a misunderstanding most of their life concerning God's character and love. Getting that cleared up will assist in discovering His loving view of you. I had a horrible misunderstanding of God's love for many years. It started at birth.

I was born into negligent and harmful circumstances. My mother was an alcoholic, and I never met my father who was a drug addict and gambler. Both spent time in prison. Knowing I was entering into an earthly rejection by my earthly parents, God still saw fit to like His own idea of me. He further chose to not just like but actually delight in me. He planted me in my sad momma's womb. For some people, this seems cruel. "Why would a loving God bring a child into those circumstances?" they ask. I asked it too at times throughout my life.

But He did not do this as a cruel joke. He had a plan. But some people, like my parents, don't follow the plan, and so His grace is interjected into the seemingly cruel situation. Instead of seeing God's provision, they choose to take up a resentment with God and blame Him for everything that goes wrong. All the while He is loving, watching, caring, intervening, waiting, and bringing into play His next step in His plan.

It was not a cruel joke when He designed my biological father's sperm to meet my mother's egg and conceive in the earth what had already been conceived in His mind as an idea. No instead of laughing and enjoying a seemingly sick joke, He instead watched over me in her womb when I'm sure abortion was an option in her circle of influence. As she lived a reckless life, God watched over me in her womb. God watched over me when my father abandoned us both. Instead of abandoning me, He stayed present with me in her womb. He saw fit to birth, ransom, love, and forgive me in advance of all the destructive ways I tried to get my own longings met throughout many years. He just needed to wait for me to see it and turn to Him.

When I was five years old, my mother took me to my aunt's house and never returned to pick me up. When my aunt took me home, all mother's things were gone. A parasite was born. It's scientific name—abandonment. Only a loving God could know parasitic longings would come as a direct result of a father who ran out and a mother who would abandon.

So He chased after me until one day He captivated my heart. And much like a pearl hidden inside a dark oyster, the beauty in my life developed over time through the damage and parasites He lovingly monitored and allowed to come into my life. Some of those parasites were anger, obesity, depression, fear, insecurity, and the drive to get approval. I craved acceptance. But there weren't enough words, gifts, and head nods to ever convince me I was really acceptable. Abandonment gnawed on me like a parasite. But a pearl was forming as that little girl waited with cravings inside the dark oyster of her life.

In God's oceanic design, a natural pearl is formed by a parasite entering into the womb-like oyster shell. Being unwanted, the parasite begins to curl up and protect itself from the oyster. The oyster host also begins to protect itself from the parasite by enclosing it with a substance called nacre. This nacre, much like God's love, covers the parasite over and over, until it becomes encased completely. In due time, this process forms a pearl. At the right time, the womb-like shell is harvested and a pearl is birthed. It takes eight to twenty years for a pearl to form in God's design.

In scientific terms used for describing the formation of a pearl, the actual oyster shell is called a host. I exist, and so do you, because Father God decided so. In order for His plan to work, He needed a physical womb—a host. He chose my mother to be the host. A cold, unwanted, but temporary assignment. A way to get me here. A God assignment.

But my willingness to accept this God perspective determines whether my heart and life become like a womb or a tomb. Wombs produce life and create a climate conducive for receiving God's love. Tombs house death and create a climate conducive for bitterness, hate, insecurity, and a life without love. Don't let a misunderstanding about God's character and love hold you back from being a womb for the forming pearl inside you. Choose life. Choose Love.

He had the idea of you. He liked it. He planted you in your mother's womb knowing there would be parasites and hurts along the way. But He stayed with you, brought you through and is speaking joy and purpose over your life. Will you let your heart be a womb—trusting that, through the difficult process, Father God longs to bring life and peace, joy, and purpose to you?

Or will your heart become a tomb hardened without hope, sinking in unwillingness to accept the One who loves you and longs to draw you out of deep water?

All pearls not yet harvested exist in deep and dark water waiting to be found. As a counselor, I have the sacred honor of walking through deep and dark water in people's hearts all the time. When God placed the call to be a counselor on my life, He did so through the following Scripture: "I will go before you and level the exalted places, I will break in pieces the doors of bronze and cut through the bars of iron, I will give you the treasures of darkness and the hoards in secret places, that you may know that it is I, the Lord God of Israel, who calls you by your name" (Isaiah 45:2–3).

Little did I know at the time, God was seeking to break and cut through the iron bars of anger, strongholds of fear, food, and self-loathing in my own heart. He would soon show me the treasure in being abandoned.

Before the foundations of the world, Father God thought of you.

> He had the idea of you, and He liked it so much that He planted you in your momma's womb knowing the difficulties you would face in this life. But He has lovingly brought you through to this day to tell you He is passionate about your presence and purpose in the world. You are a pearl of great worth. Always. Period.

Pearl in Progress, He loves you and that love is offered regardless of anything you do. It doesn't matter where you've been or even where you haven't been. He knows what has been done to you or what you have done to others. He still delights in you—even if you don't choose Him back. Just like a pearl that's forming in deep waters throughout oceans, He sees you in your own deep water trying to survive the resistant and painful circumstances flowing over you. He waits to touch your heart and reveal His love to your hurts, betrayals, and sin. His heart still longs *for you* to look for Him from where you are and to see His hand waiting to bring you up from the water to reveal you. You are a pearl of great worth in God's eyes and your name is written on His heart. Here's what He has to say to you…I love you.

Found By Love

AMERICAN CULTURE SCREAMS. Find love! Find the person you are meant to love. Cute little sayings like, "I have found the one my soul loves" hang inside most chic California boutiques. We will never find the one our soul loves until we are found by the One who unconditionally loves.

Our Soul

The soul is made up of our mind, will, and emotions. The mind and the will are the parts that are considered *voluntary*; we choose what we think in our mind and what to do with those thoughts in our mind. The emotional part of our soul is *involuntary*, meaning it's not possible to simply decide to feel angry, sad, or happy. You don't even decide to feel love. This is probably the most misunderstood part of our girl/womanhood.

Now, if we don't decide to feel love, it just happens, right? No. What most of us call love in our feelings vocabulary is not actually love at all. Many of you may say, "Yeah, my mom loves me, my dad loves me." How do you know? Are they hugging and kissing you and buying gifts all day? No. So how do you know someone loves you?

Love is not just a feeling between humans. Real and lasting love comes from Father God and all other love is subject to His love.

God's love is more like a place. It is a knowledge. A stance. It is a way of being...but not a feeling—though feelings may accompany it in varying degrees. But love, especially from Father God is not defined in a feeling. It is a profound and definitive place to discover and then a decision can be made to stay there or not.

How do you define love? Some responses I have heard are: being needed, wanting to be with someone, feeling safe, needing someone to balance me out, an intense feeling, passion, warm affection, deep sexual desire, or a positive feeling toward someone. These are elements of emotions associated with love, but these things are conditional and change with circumstances and contexts.

Unconditional Love

When the parasite enters the oyster host, it senses being unwanted and so begins to curl up and protect itself. Do you ever feel like you need a place to curl up, hide, and get comfort and rest? A place that hides you from something or someone? That uncomfortable hole you feel is where God

would run and hide. The object of the game was to get back to home base (which "it" was guarding in between chasing after people to tag them) without being tagged. Anyone who made it to home without being tagged was free and able to sit down and rest from all the running around and being chased by the enemy.

Think of God's love like that place: safe, restful, no one can touch you to knock you out of the game. Oh, and by the way, this love of God at home base is like having a perfect Father. Would you like one of those?

Examine the following list of loving characteristics found in the heart of the Perfect Father. God. Based on these truths, home base can be a shelter, refuge, dwelling, hiding because of who God is as a Perfect Father. If you allow Him to build this home base in you, you will know real and lasting love. But you must give Him permission. Will you?

1. The foundation of this love is *unconditional*. He does not decide whether or not you are loveable based on your performance. He decides to love you based on His own heart and character and best interests toward you. He dispenses grace, mercy, and justice. (See Romans 5:6–8)

2. His love is *endless* and *relentless*. It never stops. (See Romans 8:35–39, Psalm 90:14, Deuteronomy 7:6–9)

3. His love *never leaves*. Another way of saying this is that it is eternal and does not originate from the earth

or anyone on the earth. Everything on the earth is temporary so it can't be so. (Deuteronomy 31, Romans 8:37–39)

4. His love is *pure and holy*—like fire. Think about the bonfires you have been to or the fire in a fireplace. The flame itself is pure and burns through anything. Some things burn or melt more slowly depending on the substance they are made of. This holy fire is used to shape beautiful things like glass and precious metals. Its goal is to make a beautiful treasure. From godless to godly. His divine protection holds a no-tolerance policy on sin. Sin must be removed for beauty and purpose to be revealed. This is done through His pure, love work of grace, not our performance. (1 Samuel 2:2, Romans 4:5–8, Ephesians 2:8–9)

5. His love is always working in our *best interest*. (Psalms 23; Psalms 34:8, 10; Psalms 37:3–6)

6. His love is like *the power* of a swift river. It moves over and around and through the holes, rocks, and turns to shape the landscape over and under it. Forgiveness is forged as these places allow His love to wash over and through them. It changes the landscape and disposition of the river in His timing.

7. His love *lets us choose*.

8. His love *chases us* because of a longing to be with us. (Genesis to Revelation)

Reclaimed

Biblical Truth

I WILL PRAISE the Lord O my soul; all my inmost being, praise his holy name...who redeems my life from the pit and crowns me with love and compassion, who satisfies my desires with good things so that my youth is renewed like the eagle's. (Psalms 103:4–5)

Value Concept

I am a daughter of the King of Kings; I already inherited everything I need.

Battle Cry

I will reclaim what was stolen from me through lies I believed. I will believe the truth of Christ Jesus and refuse to fall for the enemy's every day attempts to break me down. I will seek to position myself in the confidence of Christ's perfect work on the cross and the empowerment it provides.

Application

Daily, conduct all my affairs while wearing my invisible crown. When I forget and it falls off, I will pick it up and put it on again.

Rescue Royale

FOUND BY LOVE, you can begin to gather the strength and energy needed to heal and *reclaim* your identity, value, and activate your inheritance. "Wait a minute, you say, how can I *re*claim something I never had in the first place?"

If you allow yourself to be fully embraced by the deep love of God and make your home in His securing acceptance and shelter, He will begin to captivate your heart. You start to trust Him more and more. His love draws you in, but His beauty as well as the beauty of how He sees and values your being will keep you there. You are captured!

In the unconditional love place, you are continuously valued, accepted, and sheltered. It is in this place you begin to understand the extravagantly high cost that affords you to be there. This understanding comes as you look at the nature of a much-needed rescue and more fully grasp the intensity of the cost involved.

The Need for Rescue

One of the most important results of God's unconditional love is security. The world wants you to gain a name and self-confidence from what you do and what you know. God's love calls you to be securely confident based on who He says you are and what He says about your best interests and well-being. But God's original design for a secure confidence was lost in the garden when Eve encountered her first enemy—Satan. The enemy slithered into a beautiful garden scene one day. We see it in Genesis 3. "So the serpent came to the woman. 'Really?' he asked. 'None of the fruit in the garden? God says you mustn't eat any of it?'" "'Of course we may eat it,' the woman told him. 'It's only the fruit from the tree at the center of the garden that we are not to eat. God says we mustn't eat it or even touch it, or we will die.'" "'That's a lie!' the serpent hissed, "You'll not die!' God knows very well that the instant you eat it you will become like him, for your eyes will be opened—you will be able to distinguish good from evil.'" "The woman was convinced. How lovely and fresh looking it was! And it would make her so wise! So she ate some of the fruit and gave some to her husband, and he ate it too. And as they ate it, suddenly they became aware of their nakedness, and were embarrassed. So they strung fig leaves together to cover themselves around the hips" (Genesis 3:1–7, TLB).

A parasitic enemy entered into a beautiful garden setting and a misunderstanding was born between God and His creation. Eve was deceived and two lies were birthed in her belief system. The first lie was this: "God is good, He loves you, but He's holding out on you. He won't give you everything you need." This was a lie to form a stronghold against the truth of who our Father truly is.

The second lie was: "Even though you are created by God, you are not enough. You need to add value to yourself in order to be valuable *enough*." This lie was meant to form a stronghold against the truth of who you are as a daughter of Father God. The instant Eve's heart repositioned to hear a different voice about her value and wisdom and yielded to something dangerous and destructive, she felt ashamed in her core. It wasn't her Father's voice. He was never critical, but loving, directing, authoritative, and full of rest and joy. This new voice she experienced in the garden was critical, authoritative, redirecting, and full of work and divisiveness. Once the bite was taken, intimacy with the deepest love possible was interrupted and Eve felt naked. To this point, the Father could always see through to her soul and, because it had no sin, it was never a problem. But now this intimacy could see sin, so there was a problem that probably felt like a hole the size of the Grand Canyon. She was so ashamed she figured out real quick how to make plants into clothes!

But that hole was not intended to be filled with guilt and condemnation, but with the deep love of the Father. His love is so full, dense, and overwhelming that sin cannot be in the presence of it without being extinguished. It's one of Satan's biggest deceptions. He wants you to believe God hates you in those sinful moments, but He doesn't. He loves you. He hates the sin and separation, but He loves you. When you are captured by the cleansing power of His love, you want to quickly return to it—not keep Him waiting. It is in this state that you have confidence before God, because your heart does not condemn. That's because His love hovers, waiting to do its perfect work. Much like Eve, a woman can do strange things when she makes someone else's voice her highest affection instead of Father's.

What do you tend on doing when someone slithers into your life and tells you in some way that you're not enough? Tells you that you need to do more in order to be acceptable? What voice is positioning itself to be your highest affection and to tell you that God is holding out on you?

Well, Eve got busy making clothes out of leaves and dressed herself and Adam. They ran and hid. They didn't just hide. They *ran* and hid. Instead of running to Father God, the very One who had the idea of them and created them in joy, they ran into the creation that was actually lower ranking than them—the trees, bushes, rocks, and whatever they could find to hide themselves. They ran from the voice they had known their whole life. The One that always loved them, spoke joy into them, and taught them how to extract life from creation for physical sustenance. The life-giver of the universe walked and talked with them every day. There was never a break in the awareness of His presence. And in this one spellbinding moment, all they could do was run into the parts of creation that were made to give them life, not hiding and secrecy.

I always thought running and hiding was an odd reaction until I had my intimate love encounter with Father God. Then I realized that once Adam and Eve knew they had momentarily and for the first time lost that intimate connection, it must have been excruciating and shocking to experience separation from Him for the first time. The unconditional and intimate love was seemingly gone—when that's all they had ever known. But it wasn't gone, just misplaced. It needed to be reclaimed.

From that point in the garden and forward, God began making a way to reclaim woman's identity, value, and purpose (and men too but they need their own book on this). He did this by sending His son Jesus to fund the rescue. It cost Father God and Jesus an extravagant price to rescue Eve from the garden kidnapping, and in doing so, reclaim any who would be reclaimed back to Himself. "Who, when He had found one pearl of great price, went and sold all that he had and bought it" (Matthew 13:46).

Change your point of view

If you view your value and identity through human sources and experiences instead of what God tells you, you will often fluctuate in your confidence and sense of well-being. The world's offerings of identity and self-image are based on human ideas and measurements which means they change all the time according to what's current in culture. When the measurement is constantly being moved, over time this will damage your ability to trust people, as well as God. As you adjust to changing expectations and image concepts, you will unnecessarily experience the pain of unmet expectations. Unmet expectations, as well as rejection, thrive outside love and intimacy with the Father.

This is what happened in the garden. Eve left her one true source that had always spoken love and value over her, and shifted momentarily to hear from another source. This source had a logical argument. God's love and whispers of value defy logic and man-made arguments. Eve got caught in the snare of believing logic instead of staying in God's love. This snare required a rescue. The pit of feeling ashamed and outwitted brought despair, shame, and guilt—a pit void of the intimacy between her and the Father. The destructive path began the moment she chose to run and hide, instead of running toward home base where love and intimacy could be restored with her Father. The shame and guilt lingered, entered into her children, and the entire system of life on earth was altered. Jeff VanVonderen says in his book, *Families Where Grace Is in Place*, that two curses came into existence that carried on until Jesus died on the cross1 (See Genesis 3). Personally, I believe the relational aspect of these curses was a result of the loss of connection with their Father.

The first curse for both Adam and Eve was a physical one. Adam's physical curse was that he would have to toil, sweat, and know the burden of work. For Eve, she would

---

1   VonVanderen, Jeff. *Families Where Grace Is in Place*

experience great pain in childbearing. But there was a subsequent relational curse for both of them. Eve would forever be wanting her husband to fill all her needs (including the ones her Father had been meeting), and he wouldn't have the capacity to. Because no man can be God to his wife or girlfriend. Adam's relationship curse would be that his wife would be forever wanting him to be her everything and knowing he couldn't. But a rescue was already formed in the heart of God. For Eve, and for you.

When your heart can believe in the One who actually had the idea of you, took pleasure in it, and then created you, then it's not a huge leap to believe that Father God would rescue you. You and God can then begin to carve out a shelter in your soul (your core) where you learn to view man-made arguments, rejection, and unmet expectations from His point of view—not the changing culture or current voice of reason.

I am sure there was much whispering over me when I was a little girl: "What is going to happen to her? Her mother is a drunk! Her daddy is no good." At other times I heard whispers about how fat I was. I was so fat in kindergarten that I couldn't do a lot of things on the playground. When I played on the seesaw, I had to have two people on the other end to balance my weight. Hearing negative whispers kept parts of me running and hiding for years. I ran from anything and anyone that would require a long-term commitment or a surrender of control. I desperately needed control in my daily circumstances to prevent me from getting into a position where I could be abandoned again. I let many rejecting words determine the direction of my life and decisions well into my thirties and even forties. I learned to please people in the smallest of things just to keep peace because if peace was lost, I thought I might get lost too.

I wanted to participate in a beauty pageant so I could get the validation I was longing for. The director of the pageant told me I had a pretty face, but the hips were going to be a problem. I wanted to be an interior designer, but math grades and teachers joking about my inability to do math kept me from even trying. I majored in something that would be safe. Most decisions, directions, and relationships were filtered through rejection and the lies I believed. A major lie I believed that set itself up against the truth of God was that He loved me out of *duty*. That's what a rescue was. When my mother abandoned me, my aunt and uncle took me into their home. For years, the lie of God's dutiful love reflected on how I received love from my aunt and uncle. On how I received love from anyone. A dutiful, martyr-style love. A dutiful rescue.

The second lie I believed was that I was not really loveable. After all, if I was loveable, why would my own mother and father abandon me? I desperately needed a rescue. Like a pearl that takes approximately eight to twenty years to form, I lived in the pain of dutiful love a long time before I encountered the unconditional love of God decades later. The remainder of this book fills in my dutiful escapades of love, but eventually I encountered His unconditional love. I gained a beautiful filtering system for those lies accumulated through the years. Meeting Him in the shelter of love place, encased in unconditional acceptance, now His love guides me lovingly to rest, not dutiful striving. Instead of criticism and duty, any needed correction is poured into me through His love.

Learning to filter pain and rejection through God's unconditional love isn't pain free, however. Have you ever considered what a different scenario it would have been if Eve and Adam would have been repented instead of running and hiding? If Eve would have ran to Father God, her known safe place, and worked it through with Him, she may have learned that it hurts to face His presence with guilt in her heart, but seeking to reconnect would have protected and restored the love and intimacy they had always had together. Love and connection reclaimed!

The presence and power of the waters washing over the oyster where a pearl lives has its job to do. In the intimate recesses of the oyster's womb, the water and grit irritatingly work with the nacre to produce its unique shimmer and one-of-a-kind unique shape. Can you see how all things, even beliefs and events that occur before a rescue, are working together to form you—the unique you with His planned shimmer?

Until the Rescue
Fake IDs

Part of the need for a rescue is birthed from the insignificance we feel. We all deal with it in various ways. But all the ways seek one thing: significance in our existence. There are many ways girls may seek to find significance and identity: sports, talent, status/image, body appearance, sexuality, personal possessions, money, career, and reputation. These measurements, due to their constant fluctuation, perpetuate a girl's tendency to become a people pleaser and a performer, always looking outward to find the right measurement reference to determine who or how to be.

If a girl equates her value and identity in being a good basketball player or a cheerleader, then she will enter an identity crisis when she doesn't do those sports anymore. When a girl attempts to find value and identity in sexuality, her terms of approval, success, and measurement will change with every boyfriend. Furthermore, if a girl is sexually abused, and more often than not this occurs over long periods of time, she becomes conditioned physically. She will be likely to choose from a whole spectrum of behaviors to try to gain value and identity, often exhibiting sexual cravings or the hatred of it altogether. Emotional pain always seeks out some sort of pleasure for comfort. It is human nature to use the road most familiar to find that comfort. So if a girl through sexual abuse becomes conditioned to need sex physically, emotionally, or for control then she will often use sex to find comfort. After being found by His love, the challenge will be for her to pursue the one true place of love, home base, over and over to break the pattern of seeking temporary comfort. Father God is our own source of individual comfort. He sent

His son to die to rescue us, but seeks to know and comfort us through a Father's intimacy and affection.

Inside the oyster, the parasite that's being covered over and over with nacre becomes one with it. Over time you cannot separate them. As a girl allows the Father's love to encase her over and over, she will *become loved*. In other words, a girl's value and identity is not based on her pain and issues. They are based on who her Father God says she is and the value His love speaks into her. He says she is a pearl of great value, and so He sent His only son to die the kind of death only known to criminals. The crucifixion in that day was the worst way to die, but the Romans used it often. It was such a shameful death that when a woman was crucified, they would hang her with her head facing inward, because it was too shameful, even for bystanders, to watch a woman die this way. Jesus, the loved son of Father God, was sent to be the love letter to the world and to you. Father's word was written *in* Jesus. Father God didn't just write a love letter, He *is* the letter *in* Jesus. His loving Father intentions were to write this love letter on our hearts.

The Ten Commandments could not tap the human heart or explain the extent of His love to the point of extravagant cost, so it had to be. We needed a rescue and the Ten Commandments couldn't buy anyone out a pit, much less change a person's identity. No, this rescue required an extravagant price due to the value of who was being rescued. Father God's children were being rescued, reclaimed for eternity. But like Eve, who ran and hid, we must come out of hiding and choose to be found and rescued. His kind of love doesn't force anyone out of hiding—only loves us out.

So it is with Father God's love covering a sexually abused girl over and over to become One with her. If she chooses to come out of hiding and accept the nacre of God's love and lets herself be found in it over and over, He will satisfy her more than all the touches possible through mere physical human touch and sexuality. His loving presence is able to penetrate all parts of her being: body, soul, and spirit. It is like a sweetly discharged explosion of the purest form of love known. It has been said that water always seeks the lowest point to fill. The deepest form of violation against a girl is sexual abuse. His presence, like liquid love, will go to her lowest point and satisfy its parched ground. A pearl must have water to exist. A girl must have her Father's love to thrive.

Rejoice Royale

The Lord your God in your midst, The Mighty One, will save; He will rejoice over you with gladness. He will quiet you with His love. He will rejoice over you with singing.

—Zephaniah 3:17

COULD ANYONE REJOICING with gladness and singing do so without a smile on their face? Father smiles on you. Imagine His smile over you while you were being knit together in your momma's womb. Imagine His smile over you when you were born! Imagine His smile over you. Imagine the creator of the universe hovering over His ocean waters, enjoying its beauty and life-nurturing qualities, delighting in the beautiful pearls which are silently, but powerfully forming inside tiny shell wombs. How much more will He then be hovering in your midst, waiting to rescue you, rejoicing over His own idea of you and that you are in Him? His presence and being *is* love, and so it is in His presence that your angst and striving to be enough is finally quieted.

It is here in this quieted presence you find that you are finally enough. As He rejoices over you and, like a daddy cradling his restless toddler, begins to sing over you. His presence would have been plenty, but His singing fills your soul with the knowledge you are delighted in.

I believe this is what Peter is talking about in 1 Peter 3:3–4: "Do not let your adornment be merely outward-arranging the hair, wearing gold, or putting on fine apparel-rather let it be the hidden person of the heart, with the incorruptible beauty of a gentle and quiet spirit, which is very precious in the sight of God." This passage is not a fashion-bashing passage. It's telling us what emphasis is precious to our Father. The heart.

When He quiets us with His love (Zephaniah 3:17), it calms our spirit, and the voices that drive us to strive and seek to be somebody we aren't begin to fade and eventually banish. The need for hair arrangements, designer labels, and fine houses take a lower priority. In fact, they become viewed as blessings, not entitlements. We find in His presence that we are enough, and we are quieted. Because we have ceased angst in our inner being, we can actually sense or even hear Him singing over us. We know we are loved, and all the world is right from that center point. Oh, to be so quieted by His love in the dark and deep places of life that we can experience His rejoicing over us in our midst. The fact that Creator God looks directly into you and speaks love creates a melody beyond any love composition known.

Heiress Royale

FOUND IN HIS love and rescued by an extravagant price, we can begin reclaiming things that Satan stole to harm us and benefit his evil agenda. What God intended for beauty, pure pleasure, and eternal purpose, like sex, for example, Satan will seek to steal, kill, and destroy. That's the heart of reclaiming. Taking back what was God's gift to us in the first place. But taking it back His way.

Lianna was insecure due to a low view of her intellect and body type. She thought she needed to have a certain sex appeal to be considered beautiful. She had a hard time keeping up with her friends who achieved school awards and excellent grades. She began to try to make up for this insecurity. Each time a boy paid attention to her, she tried really hard to keep that boyfriend as proof that she was valuable. She used him to feel secure. When the boy finally became obsessed with her, she would dump him because she needed to make sure she was still getting the approval of other available guys. She would go find another guy to prove something to, in hopes of gaining some sense of value for her existence.

Much like trophies on a shelf for the jock, relationships came and went starting at age thirteen, earning her a young life full of trophy hearts she had achieved and broken to prove she was a valuable commodity. Eventually, a pattern was so established that she couldn't commit to anyone. She became obsessed with the feeling of fresh love and the actual drive to get a guy's approval. She was addicted to getting in and out of relationships in order to seek out something that she could never get her hands on: Love. Identity. Value.

True identity lies in who our loving Creator says we are and the value He places on us. He never changes and so, if we fix our gaze on Him, our terms of approval and measurement won't either. Instead, it lays a foundation we can stand on for true value and identity. John Piper says, "What gives us our identity is not color or culture, but chosenness."[1]

"Who, when He had found one pearl of great price, went and sold all that he had and bought it" (Matt. 13:46).

Abraham's sperm did not give Isaac His identity as the one God promised. It was God's promise that gave Isaac his identity as the chosen one of Israel. Your father's sperm did not give you your identity, nor did your abuser. God did. So go get it! Go reclaim it. Cut loose those people, experiences, and patterns Satan has been using to tell you who you are,

---

1   Piper, John.

and reclaim it! *Take back* your stolen identity. Scream it out. "You don't tell me who I am. Only God does."

Who does He say I am?
Original

Have you ever received something handmade by someone who chose you for a friend? It usually has a higher value to both the giver and the receiver when hands have made something personal. It is valuable to the giver because of the time, resources, and talent that was spent on making it. The very idea of creating something just for you is what makes it valuable. If their own hands made it, and they put their heart into it then it's as though you have a piece of them with you as long as you have the gift. Every time you pick up the gift you are noting that you have been identified or associated with this person in a personal way. This is the way it is with our identity in Christ.

My daughter Gabrielle creates beautiful handmade greeting cards and invitations. I keep all of them because each one is unique and different and given for a different reason. And it's true even if there is a pattern involved and she makes multiples. The colors she chooses may vary, or the mood, or even the process she used may change as she completes each one. I have never received two alike. These little treasures help me feel loved by her because I know she took time to give herself in the creation process with her thoughts of me as she did it.

Unique

When God created you He was thinking of you and Himself. He had the idea of you, delighted in His idea, and planted you in your mother's womb to be brought forth in due time. Every girl has her own unique set of fingerprints…as though handmade. I read an article recently about identical twins. They are identical even in their DNA. But when it came to fingerprinting them, they were unique from each other.

Royal Inheritance

I have an heirloom. It is a quilt made by a great-grandmother I never met. It is old and a bit tattered, but the fabric, thread, and pattern reflect the hands and heart of a woman whose bloodline give me parts of how I look, behave, and think. People who knew her can probably see it in my hands, the way my mouth moves when I talk, and my natural disposition. Now how would I know that having never met her? I have seen pictures, heard the stories, and I feel the connection to her daughter which is my grandmother. My grandmother received the quilt after her mother made it. I acquired it from her. I treasure the quilt because of where it came from and the lineage it bears. My identity is threaded throughout the lineage to its origin. It belongs to me because in its very essence, it bears my heritage.

An Heiress

Here's another way of saying it. I am an heiress and received a quilt through my bloodline to the quilter. Like the worn and tattered quilt, I belong to Father God's bloodline, and my life is valuable simply because of the One who created it. And then when it was lost, Jesus spilt His blood as Father's payment to get it back. God's heart and all its resources, especially regarding His son Jesus, are my true treasures... my inheritance. Calvin Miller says in his book, *Letting Go,* "When we confessed our sin and accepted Christ's life giving sacrifice we traversed the birth canal to become significant." 2 You are His heiress and belong to this bloodline the minute you choose to. He had the idea of you, liked it, rescued you, and invited you to reclaim your connection and eternal resources from Him. Your inherent value was kidnapped along the way, but because your value originated with Him, He paid an extravagant price to reclaim it for you through Jesus's work on the cross. He simply asks that you come to Him to reclaim what Satan sabotaged from your ancestor, Eve, and all women.

The quilt story illustrates the Creator, created, inheritance, and value, but this inheritance is royal, eternal, and more than a quilt. Psalm 16:5–6 says, "You are the portion of my inheritance and my cup; you maintain my lot. The lines have fallen for me in pleasant places. Yes, I have a good inheritance."

---

2   Miller, Calvin. Letting Go

I love reading about these lines falling in pleasant places through Scripture as they describe my inheritance. Unlike today, when lawyers have several-feet high stacks of paper to describe what possessions family members acquire upon a loved one's death, my inheritance and yours can be read in the following precious and condensed lines, like love notes from a dad to His adopted daughter.

> My dear daughter,
>
> I am delighted to inform you that the inheritance I have acquired for you is complete and now ready to be activated. According to my will, the following line items are ready for you to take possession of, activate, and enjoy your entire life. I am your daddy! I have waited for you to come to my royal table and see all that I have reserved for you.

I created you in my own image. "So God created man in his own image, in the image of God he created him; male and female he created them" (Gen. 1:27, ESV).

I have adopted you because I love you. "For you did not receive the spirit of slavery to fall back into fear, but you have received the Spirit of adoption as sons, (or daughter) by whom we cry, 'Abba! Father!'" Rom. 8:15 (emphasis mine).

You have a new life! You can start fresh! Here! Take it! This means that anyone who belongs to Christ has become a new person. The old life is gone; a new life has begun! (2 Cor. 5:17).

You have Love for the rest of your life, no matter what happens. "For I am sure that neither death nor life, nor angels nor rulers, nor things present nor things to come, nor powers, nor height nor depth, nor anything else in all creation will be able to separate us from the love of God in Christ Jesus our Lord" (Romans 8:37–39).

You have been reclaimed from a life of orphan-hood and a life of living off scraps! I am always with you. "Fear not, for I have redeemed you; I have called you by name, you are mine. When you pass through the waters, I will be with you; and through the rivers, they shall not overwhelm you; when you walk through fire you shall not be burned, and the flame shall not consume you. For I am the Lord your God" (Isa. 43:1–3, ESV).

I have dressed you like a royal daughter! "He has clothed me with the garments of salvation; he has covered me with the robe of righteousness, as a bridegroom decks himself like a priest with a beautiful headdress, and as a bride adorns herself with her jewels" (Isa. 61:10, ESV).

I release to you all these benefits: Forgiveness, healing, a life that's paid for, a beautiful crown to wear at all times, complete satisfaction with continuous and renewable strength. "Forget not all his benefits, who forgives all your iniquity, who heals all your diseases, who redeems your life from the pit, who crowns you with steadfast love and mercy who satisfies you with good so that your youth is renewed like the eagle's. I love you. Your Abba Daddy."

This abandoned girl is no longer abandoned! I am not an orphan. I love my inheritance and the benefits of it. It satisfies the gnawing parasite. But even the beautiful crown, satisfaction, new life, forgiveness, and emotional healing aspects of this beautiful inheritance do not compare to the One who gives it. I have come to want Him even more than the inheritance.

Affection

How lovely is your dwelling place, O Lord of hosts!
My soul longs, yes, faints for the courts of the Lord;
my heart and flesh sing for joy to the living God.
Even the sparrow finds a home, and the swallow a
nest for herself, where she may lay her young, at your
altars, O lord of hosts, my King and my God.

—Psalm 84:1–3

Value Concept

HE WANTS TO have an intimate relationship with me.

Battle Cry

I will regard God in Christ Jesus as my highest affection
in devotion and decisions where He will open His heart
intimately to me and He will show me my daily path.

Application

I will keep my heart so attached to Jesus that a boy has to go through Him to get to me.

With Highest Affection

Wombs or Tombs

OYSTERS FILTER UP to five liters of water each day. Water is a life-giving element in the making of a pearl. As a human, your body thirsts for water, but your soul and spirit are made to long for living water.

Whatever your heart longs for reveals your true affections, and depending on what they are, comprise a womb or tomb atmosphere in your heart. Do you long for living water or thirst for things that only make you spiritually parched? Living water nurtures the presence of life. Dehydration is evidence of water depletion. This can lead to physical death in some cases, but certainly leads to spiritual death. Longing for the love and presence of God, like living water, will determine whether you ever discover the living source of your value and purpose.

Affection is that deep and tender longing for something or someone. There is a certain affection that creates a womb-like climate in your heart for housing the love and presence of God. He longs to be the highest affection in your heart. Reserving a deep and tender longing for Him above all other loves creates a womb-like atmosphere to grow in fullness of Him. But He waits to be wanted. Stephanie Tucker, author of *The Christian Codependence Workbook,* says "Our Heavenly Father is a gentleman. He never forces himself on anyone." 1 His love is not dependent on our performance, but is most often experienced because of our willing and affectionate invitation from the inside. He waits to be wanted.

It is extremely important to understand that misplaced affections don't change His viewpoint of you. He still loves and rejoices over your existence, even from a distance. But seeking to hold Him in your heart's most tender place nurtures the connection from your heart to His. The door of our hearts, so to speak, has a doorknob on the inside, not on the outside. He doesn't barge in, He waits to be wanted. His heart can open up and reveal grace and love to us any time He wants because He's God. But revelation in your head alone doesn't usher it in. You must *receive* the revealed grace and love into your heart.

Receiving His love and grace enables your heart to create a climate of affection for Father God. A girl who longs after His heart, who longs for intimacy with him, will soon be a vessel of love, humility, surrender, and trust. This is the

---

1   Tucker, Stephanie. *The Christian Codependence Workbook.*

symbiotic climate where Father loves to hang out and is free to speak, guide, and direct. This embryonic climate becomes a dwelling place for God's presence to swell in large proportion, spilling out onto everyone it comes into contact with.

These affections not only create a climate for His presence to dwell, but they also enable a lovely atmosphere for Father God to reveal very personal and intimate details concerning your true identity and eternal value.

When Melody experienced God's healing from years of abuse from a deacon in her church, the affections in her heart changed. She was a Christian, but had chosen self-destructive activities like alcohol binges and one-night stands to numb the pain of her shame. Other women who had learned to hold Father as their highest affection spoke and prayed into her life. The love and presence they housed was poured into her heart and served to demonstrate His love and grace. The consistency and lack of judgment in the living water kept pouring in, and gradually she experienced her thirst being truly satisfied. The love and grace removed the shame as she gradually activated her trust in God's ability to remove it. She began to have the longing for more of this God who saw her inner mess and demonstrated love and grace instead of shame and guilt. Melody grew to learn He was more worthy of her affection than alcohol, one-night stands, and her closet of masks, masquerades, and numbing devices. Her affection for Him ushered in truth from His point of view: She is valuable. She longed for more of Him. And the more she did, the more

He revealed Himself to her. In the growing revelations, she was found—the true Melody. She found deep acceptance. God's presence swelled to great proportions in her life. Now she also houses His love and presence and it splashes onto those around her.

During the course of her journey, Melody learned to value what God values. Because He valued her, she scheduled a medical appointment to be tested for STDs. While she had none, the doctor told her she would never have children. Today Melody is married to a loving man, and they have two beautiful children. Making Him your highest affection creates a life-giving climate. Will you choose to develop the following affections in the innermost parts of your heart? If so, they will serve to produce a life-giving climate, like a womb.

Longing for Him

Want Him More

THINK OF YOUR favorite person in the world. It might be your spouse, a friend, your child, a teacher, a parent, family member, or elderly person. When you sense their presence you are so excited you just want to be near them or at least be in the same room with them. Their presence does something to you. Their presence opens up a desire to hear what they are going to say. When they are in the room speaking to someone else, you find yourself trying to get as close as you can to the conversation so you can hear them, their ideas, their tone, and the message of what they are saying. You long for their presence to turn and speak directly to you, and when they do, it is as though you are the only one in the room.

Oftentimes, this is the way a girl feels about a boy when she starts liking him. Or a woman for a man. But Father longs for us to want him first and more. Oh, I know you can't physically see Him or what He is wearing like you can a boy. But for your soul (core) development, it is extremely important to develop a longing for Father even though you can't see Him in the same way. Developing an affection of longing for Father more than anyone else prepares you for true earthly love. You embrace that, while it's okay to be infatuated with a boy, the goal is to be more infatuated with the presence of Father. Longing for His presence will put you in a healthy position to hear from Him, especially concerning the boy—that is *if* you want to hear from Him about the boy! If not, then heart satisfaction concerning that boy will always be slightly out of reach. Our hearts were made to long for Father *more*, and to be satisfied by Him first—then the boy.

In all creation, there is a built-in longing for life. Developing an affection of longing for Father and what He offers us more than anything else in the world is life giving! But it doesn't bring life quickly. Like the pearl in an oyster womb, beautiful fruit requires time, tender care, and waiting to come into its harvest.

When a woman carries a baby in her womb, she longs to see the life that's being created; first, with an ultrasound, then through the beautiful growth of her belly. She dreams about the final face-to-face meeting that comes after nine months of longing. But it will cost her; beautiful babies come with a cry, a lot of sweat, and pain in places you never knew you had.

God placed life-giving energy in His nature through the process of nutrients which defy gravity and come up from the ground to the stem and bud to birth a bloom. Just before a rose blooms, the bud longs to open up and receive sunshine and offer its beauty to the world. It longs to be revealed, but if it starts to open before its time, it dies off without ever fully opening.

Have you ever thought about the time and patience in that life-giving process? We often walk right by such things without even thinking about the invisible life-giving acceptance the rose plant has for God's life-giving birth process. You can't hear an audible presence in the life of a growing rose, you can only see the result of it. But what separates us from creation is that we are made in His image and for relationship. Not only can our bodies bring forth life, but we have the privilege of housing spirit life through the Holy Spirit. This presence is worth longing for.

Longing for His Voice

How do you learn to hear this amazing voice? It begins with longing for His presence and the voice will become discernible. Making Him your highest affection will serve to reposition yourself for an intimate relational pattern with Father. This will enable you to gain hearing abilities. You will discover the following discernible qualities in His voice.

His voice speaks truth. Always. Develop a tender affection toward this presence of truth. Long to hear the truth about how He views you. You can begin to hear your Heavenly Father speak value over you as you decrease the power of the enemy's voice calling you to compare yourself to others, or to please the hard-to-please people. Why are we so quick to listen to the negative and life-sucking voices over the life-giving presence and voice of Father God? Because it's easier. The enemy's voice is coming from several sources: the media, the jealous friend, the resentful parent, the critical coach, and the pressurized emotionally unavailable spouse. The voice of your Heavenly Father comes from His presence placed in you, it doesn't yell. Critical people yell. Negative forces seem to scream! He speaks the truth in love and with affection! Which voice do you want to have the highest affection for?

The more you spend time finding out what He says is true about you, the more skill you will gain in determining a lie about you. You become what you think. You become what you put in. Put in lies, you live one. Put in love, you live as a lover. Put in truth, you are true. It is a lovely thing to begin having so much affection toward your Father that you actually desire to daily place your thought life, decisions, and emotions into His hands. Choosing to agree and align them with God's heart of love and personal value toward you is the heart's path to peace and true beauty.

Remember the first time you fell in love? You thought of him all the time. You went places where you knew he would be. You may have even done drive-bys. Did you practice writing your name with his last name just to see how it would look? Did you write him love notes? Surprise him with gifts? I thought of him when I first woke up and he was the last one I talked to before I shut my eyes at night. With modern technology, people fall asleep talking to each other on the phone, creating astronomical cell phone bills. I wanted to wear his ring, wear his leather jacket, and, yes, at times I wanted to give my whole being to him.

I just described how someone becomes your highest affection.

Father longs for us to respond to Him that way. Think of Him all the time. Hang out where He (real love) hangs out. You can't exactly do a drive-by but you can look for God sightings—people and places where He is at work. Write Him love notes. Surprise Him with a gift by giving anonymously to someone in need. It delights Him, and He says it is unto Him when we give a drink of water to someone in need. When you wake up in the morning, picture the love of your life sitting at your bed just staring at you and waiting for you to wake up because he's crazy about you. When you lay your head down at night, picture your pillow being his lap where he sits with you in love and solitude. His presence whispers, "Rest, my darling. I loved our day together. I'll be here when you wake."

I know what some of you are thinking. You say this is ridiculous. I am reducing him to humanity by placing him in a lover role. So what was the crucifixion? A majestic and sovereign event for sure, but it was deeply personal, and without Father being the lover of your soul, Jesus would have never agreed. Because Jesus held His Father in the highest place of affection and Father loves you, then Jesus also died as the lover of your soul. They are one. Intimate.

One parasite crawls into a shell, is covered in nacre, and becomes one with it. Intimately knit together, love, and parasite form a pearl of great value. One broken girl crawls into the presence of God, encounters His love there, and finds Him to be the One worthy of her deepest and highest affection.

Perhaps your church life and upbringing made you think Christianity was a white-knuckle kind of process. Suck it up and obey God! He loves you, so you owe Him! Go to Bible study! Go to youth! Go to camp! Go! Go! Do, Do, Do! Develop an affection for the Father above other affections. Develop an affection for the presence of your Father. Jesus said it this way, "But seek ye first the kingdom of God, and His righteousness; and all these things shall be added unto you" (Matt. 6:33, KJV). The kingdom of God is found in the heart of God as revealed through His written word, His presence and voice. The kingdom of God is an affection issue long before it became a behavior issue.

His voice speaks value. Always. With Father, no consumerism resides in His heart. He doesn't use His created. He enjoys it. Sustains it. He never throws away His glory. He never defaces His own image. It is always beautiful and the desire to redeem it casts shadows on the whole idea of using you or tossing you to the dumpster.

We live in a consumer-driven relationship world. Actual songs like *Jar of Hearts* by Christina Perri expose the enemy's scheme to drive mankind to treating each other like collector's items on a shelf in the lab of love and romance. Here are some everything in it, whether you want Him to or not. But as I stated earlier, He does not barge in to what He sees.

He's not afraid of the mess in there, but He does want to take an intimate walk through your heart *with* you. Father doesn't want to be invited into your messy heart so He can throw a fit and cram everything into its proper place. He longs to show you how much He cares and loves you in the midst of the mess. He will reveal matters to you that only He and you can understand together. When He takes an intimate walk through your heart with your permission, it is the beginning of the best love story you will ever live. There is nothing this side of heaven more satisfying than knowing the God of the universe has walked gently through your heart, looking tenderly and grievously at the messes, touching each one to redeem and restore it, and still accepts you. He sees clear through your complexion, your body, the shape and color of your hair, how you walk and talk, and gazes upon your core; the eternal design and value on the inside. The place where you choose truth or lies. The place where you have holes. The place where you loathe yourself.

He sees it all and accepts you just as you are. He doesn't have the attitude of a fixer. His deep love and acceptance moves Him to desire restoration for you. There's a difference between fixing and restoring.

He longs to restore you to your original design and purpose. If I found a hole in the heirloom quilt, I could fix it by covering the hole with wire mesh, pantyhose, or a denim phrases from her heart-wrenching battle cry to keep what light she finally found at the end of a dark and consumer-minded relationship. "Who do you think you are running around leaving scars collecting your jar of hearts....and I've learned to live half-alive and now you want me one more time? Who do you think you are? It took so long just to feel alright...you broke all your promises, and now you're back but you don't get to get me back."[1]

He doesn't use you. He values you. Barbie dolls are made of plastic. You aren't. Leftovers go in Styrofoam carryout containers. You don't. Would you rather drink a beautiful glass of pink lemonade in a Styrofoam container or a sun sparkled glass one? Drink tea from a paper cup? No, beautiful china teacup! What does the voice you are currently most affectionate toward say about your value?

He always speaks value and did so when He spoke through Jesus saying, "Who, when he had found one pearl of great price, went and sold all that he had and bought it."[2]

His voice speaks intimate acceptance. Always.

David and Teresa Ferguson, the authors of *Intimate Encounters*, describe intimacy as *in to me see*.[3] God sees all the way to your heart because that is His first priority. He see

---

1   "Jar of Hearts" (Perri, Christina. 2010) Track #6, Perri, Lawrenc Yeretsian. Lovestrong. Retrieved from Metrolyrics.com.

2   Holy Bible. Matthew 13:45–46, ESV.

3   Ferguson, David and Theresa. *Intimate Encounters.*

"I want to love your friend. Let me love through you."

'They are hurting. Have compassion."

"Don't judge. Just love, remembering you have been there before. "

"I'm waiting for you."

"I'm so glad you turned around and reached out to me."

"I have a plan. Don't run. Walk with me and I will show you."

"No hiding. I see you. Let me lift your head. There is no shame – just choose me from now on."

"Yes I heard you. Will you let me show you my way? I have a plan. Don't run. Walk with me and I will show you."

Read the following prayer to confirm your desire to recognize His voice and presence.

Heavenly Father, I recognize that I have been listening to many different voices. Some are louder than others, but I notice that many of them have an element of deceit in them. I long to hear your voice of love, truth, care, and real direction. Train my core. Be my trainer God, to challenge me every day to present myself to you. I want to be strengthened in my beliefs; I want to trust you with all the details of my life, and this begins with longing for your presence to be sweeter and your voice louder than all the rest. I need your help in order to embrace and live life to its fullest. I desire to be a girl who is a lovely host to your presence-to be a beautiful pearl just like you planned since before the foundations of the world. I long to recognize your voice and your presence. Amen.

Delight

OSWALD CHAMBERS SAYS in *My Utmost for His Highest*, "The natural heart is in danger until it is satisfied in God first."[1] This is the highest and most important affection for all of life; delighting in Him. When we regard Him as the most worthy pursuit, the Holy Spirit will work in chorus with it to protect us against frivolous heart pursuits. How can we possibly go wrong with delighting in the One who had the idea of us in the first place? He knows us best. And He certainly knows why we are here.

If you bought a pair of heels at Nordstrom, would you take them to Payless to get repaired? No, because Payless has a different mindset when they make shoes. They make them cheaply! If you received a Coach purse for a gift, would you trade it for a Target brand? Target wouldn't do it! They don't want the responsibility of such a fraudulent trade! If your

---

1 Chambers, Oswald. My Utmost for His Highest Devotional

beach cruiser bike was wrecked, would you take it to an auto mechanic? I heard a girl tell a story of going into an upper end cosmetic store. She asked for a certain brand of lipstick, and the sales clerk nearly took her out with her tone and words! "We don't sell that here!"

In almost all cases, the manufacturer is the one who provides the product's directions for use and repair. Your manufacturer is God. In a world so hung up on brands and quality, why do we sell our very souls so cheaply to the shenanigans that come along? Wake up! God knows the way you work and He can heal you when you need it. Delight in His ways concerning you. He is the only one worthy of your pure and sheer delight! His heart is perfect and His care, justice, and plans are perfect for you. Delighting in Him leads to peace. Read the progression in Psalm 37 where David worships God under the pressure of someone seeking to destroy him. "Delight yourself in the Lord, and He will give you the desires of your heart." And the chapter goes on to describe how God provides as we learn to delight in Him and commit our ways. "Fret not yourself because of evildoers; be not envious of wrongdoers! For they will soon fade like the grass and wither like the green herb. Trust in the Lord, and do good; dwell in the land and befriend faithfulness. Delight yourself in the Lord, and he will give you the desires of your heart. Commit your way to the Lord; trust in him, and he will act. He will bring forth your righteousness as the light, and your justice as the noonday.

Be still before the Lord and wait patiently for him; fret not yourself over the one who prospers in his way, over the man who carries out evil devices! Refrain from anger, and forsake wrath! Fret not yourself; it tends only to evil, for the evildoers shall be cut off, but those who wait for the Lord shall inherit the land. In just a little while, the wicked will be no more; though you look carefully at his place, he will not be there. But the meek shall inherit the land and delight themselves in abundant peace." Why will He give you the desires of your heart when you delight in Him the most? Because He knows what your heart desires! He made it! But what we often think are desires are mostly lusts and cravings of the flesh. Attention, approval, closeness with someone, sexual desire, power for gaining outcomes, material gain. Etc. Those aren't the true desires of our heart. They are cravings.

So what is a true desire? True desires are the things He placed in you that could only be satisfied by Him. So how does a girl set out to be satisfied in God first, to really delight in Him? Well, there's bad news and good news about this. First, I'll give you the good news. We have already established that the God of the universe has taken delight in the very idea of you and followed through with that idea. Remember the last time you went to get frozen yogurt? You filled your cup with luscious, creamy, sweet, and tangy flavors and then crowned it with amazing embellishments of sour, sweet, chocolaty yumminess. You were in full anticipation as you went through the line taking delight in what you were about to receive: Satisfaction of your eyes, your taste buds, and your stomach! And after getting full, you were already delighting in the fact that when you came back an hour later, or even a day later, there would be more frozen yogurt. However, have you ever poured so much into that cup that you couldn't eat it all? Your capacity for delight was bigger than your tummy could handle?

Similarly, the God of the universe has delight to give you in appropriate increments for the rest of your life as you reach out for it. He is your portion! (Psalm 16:1–9) Imagine having the entire frozen yogurt shop in your garage at home and at your fingertips when you are ready to be delighted! That's the way God's heart is! He's ever present in hunger and longings for something sweet, and also when we are emotionally depleted.

While frozen yogurt seems like a frivolous example, the message is serious. He wants you to know that He desires to delight you with His promises, His presence, and His shelter of love as you develop the affection of delighting in Him and His plans and purpose.

The beauty of this is that while you are sleeping, the delight is still waiting for you when you wake up. The frozen yogurt shop in the garage didn't move or take off in the middle of the night. Like frozen yogurt in the garage, He is there waiting to delight you when you wake up. You simply get up and instead of accepting mere oats, you go to the heart of hearts to your delight and receive your supply for your morning need. This affection has served to change my life almost more than any of the others.

Now for the bad news: in order to get to the garage where the frozen yogurt is, we have to do some things to get there. First, we have to get out of bed and *wake up*. In waking up, we realize fully what our choices are. Jesus will be the first delight of the day, or it will be all the other stuff that cries out to us when we first wake up.

Delighting in Him means we have to pass up all the little and big things that call out to us on the way to the garage to receive our delight. Like giant boxes full of things we have stored in a real garage, there can be obstacles in our heart to step around or over in our pursuit of getting to the place (person) we delight in. Delight will be blocked if these two obstacles are in the way: resentments and pride.

Resentments serve as obstacles. They can be like a giant box in your heart…a storage place to keep resentments all wrapped up. Like the boxes in your garage, if you don't get it unpacked and put away, you will keep stumbling over it or adjusting around it. You can find adorable labels, markers, and all kinds of cute things to put on boxes these days to make them more attractive, but the truth is resentments are meant to be temporary, not permanent, furnishings. In addiction recovery, it is said that resentments are the seeds that sprout from unmet expectations.

Pride blocks the ability to find delight in Him. If you are hurt by the fact that only He can do for you what you cannot do for yourself, then pride is convincing you to be strong and resourceful *on your own*. Pride says to rely on your own self. Delight says be humble and receive. In light of the frozen-yogurt-in-the-garage example, pride tells you to figure out how to make frozen yogurt in the kitchen with your own hands instead of simply going out to the garage to receive delightful frozen yogurt that's already made from His hand. Much like the wall separating the house from the garage, a wall in your heart can separate your stubborn will from His delightful gifts.

The following lies may be embedded in your stubborn will, and if so, will definitely block you from spiritual growth and the ability to delight in Jesus:

- I must have immediate gratification and fulfillment of my needs and wants.
- I must avoid uncomfortable situations.
- I must be treated fairly at all times.
- I must always seek to have enough control to get things to turn out right.
- I must have approval at all times.
- I must be outstanding at everything, or I won't do it at all.
- God wants me to be happy.

Let's take this to another level. Delighting in Him means we learn to make Him our highest affection. The two terms—

delight and affection—are often reduced to material, sexual, and physical lust. You see commercials about underwear, juicy hamburgers, and cars that are able to give you everything you want. But like the frozen yogurt, these things will all pass away over time. These things aren't what gives your core substance. Consistently and intentionally placing Jesus as your highest affection will give you substance, confidence, and identity. Long for Him. Delight in Him. Place Him as the highest affection in your heart. A. W. Tozer said, "All that feeds the flesh weakens the Spirit." Learn to speak to your core, *want Him more*, in those lusting moments.

Trust

AN OLD HYMN says it well, "I dare not trust the sweetest frame, But wholly trust in Jesus's name." What is your sweetest frame in life? The question implies we are trusting in some earthly structure or relationship to make us happy and whole. Is it your husband's affection? Is it your boyfriend's attention? Do you need your children to be problem free to feel whole and free? Are you longing for an earthly resolve to give you peace? We dare not trust the sweetest frame, because in doing so, we will lose touch with His presence and will certainly suffer consequences when we make our home outside His delight and plan. Wholly trusting in Jesus's name will make us whole regardless of the external circumstances.

Trust

Trust has everything to do with confidence. If a girl has confidence in her*self* to create, be a top performer, gain popularity, compete, throughout time she may become confused with the ever-changing reference points used to measure and define these things. The world's measurement standards are constantly changing. Don't get me wrong, a pearl is confident! She lives, moves, and has her relationships from a point of inner confidence. But true and lasting confidence doesn't come from her *self*-achievements.

What are you doing while you're reading this? Are you laying on your bed? Sitting on your favorite chair, enjoying a cup of tea with a Christian sister? Sitting cross-legged on the floor or at a desk? Regardless of how your body is positioned right now, believe me, *trust* is involved. Trust that props you up securely can only come from one place. It is Father, through His son, Jesus. Whatever you are sitting, standing, or laying on is where you have transferred your personal confidence for being propped up right now. This personal transfer has another name! Trust.

A chair: you have to place your confidence in all the legs. A couch: you have to place your confidence in the springs/ support underneath to know it will hold you. A floor: you have to place your confidence in the structure of the floor as it is attached to the framework of the bigger structure it is housed in. The ground outside: you have to place your confidence in the way the universe holds together to form a solid standing place. The list goes on. But when you actually sit in the chair as opposed to looking at it and figuring it out, you have crossed over to surrender. You trust, then choose to surrender your entire body to be held by the chair. *Trust*

*is placing your confidence in what holds you together and props
you up.*

Surrender is activating that confidence by offering your
entire heart, life circumstances, and needs into the One who
holds your life. He is much more worthy than a simple chair.

All the items I mentioned have something in common.
Their structured design is subject to a larger universal pattern:
gravity and mathematical engineering as related to gravity,
balance and weight, etc. We trust because we know the
authority behind the thing in them is being trusted. In the
physical sense, it's the engineer of a chair. In the spiritual
sense, it's the Father's design.

Practicing surrender strengthens your ability to trust.
It's letting go and letting Father do for you what only He
can do. Trust practiced over time deepens your affection.
Experiencing what He can do for you and through you only
makes you want more of Him. The deeper the trust, the more
tender the affection becomes.

A trusting affection doesn't just throw trust around to
anyone however. Trust in the One who is worthy demonstrates
that you have become knowledgeable about what greater
things hold the minor things together. So it is between you
and your Heavenly Father. You may not understand the
concepts behind how all things hold together any more than
you understand the engineering behind couch design. But
you can trust the One who supplied the physics behind couch
design. Physics, engineering, and design didn't originate with

a physicist, engineer, or designer! They simply tapped into the truth about how things hold together beautifully! You too can tap into and prove Him to be your worthy life designer! You will discover His design is worthy and most definitely found to be sturdy, practical, and especially comforting in times of need. We can read about this trust in 1 Peter 1:7–9 where he speaks of Jesus Christ, "Though you have not seen him, you love him. Though you do not now see him, you believe in him and rejoice with joy that is inexpressible and filled with glory, obtaining the outcome of your faith, the salvation of your souls." An affection of trusting in what or who you can't see is life-giving and will serve to stand you up in your core.

Humility

Honestly, this is a simple idea because a truly humble person doesn't usually complicate things too much. They consider every good thing a gift and that it comes from God. Humble people know they aren't God, not the center of it all, and definitely not in charge. They know they didn't create gravity and the substance of the universe. And they know they can't hold all of it together. But even more than that, a humble person loves His presence and that it comes when she humbles herself.

"Toward the scorners He is scornful, but to the humble He gives favor" (Prov. 3:34)

"You save a humble people, but your eyes are on the haughty to bring them down" (2 Sam. 22:28).

"Humble yourself before the Lord, and he will exalt you" (James 4:10).

A humble spirited girl has an unassuming disposition. Decisions aren't made based on a hidden list of entitlements. An orphan mind-set is desperate, resentful, and feels entitled.

Humble (attitude of an heiress)	**Entitled** (attitude of an orphan)
Inner beauty/security	Worldly pursuit of outer beauty
True inner identity	Driver's license, labels, brands
Waiting on God's plan	Boy/ring by spring
Home within financial means	Model home
True friends/authenticity	Popularity
Contentment	Happiness
Christ-centered choices	Driven by personal gain / Get ahead
Godly sorrow/grief	Worldly sorrow, pity
Children are a blessing through birth, adoption, foster, or custodial	Personal trophy, little version of me

When a girl trains herself to be humble, the next attitude won't be as difficult to develop in her will.

Father,

I am finally recognizing what it means to be your precious daughter. You have paid the ultimate sacrifice to ransom my life, and now you want to simply love and provide for me, as well as protect me from what ultimately harms me. I see that I have placed other affections higher than you in my heart. I do have an attitude of entitlement concerning _____ _____.

I am choosing to repent of that affection and attitude. I choose instead to keep it simple, and know that any and all gifts you would be so kind to give me are perfect and sufficient. I long for you more. I release my feelings of entitlement. I desire to keep myself bowed down before you in confidence, not shame. I am in grateful awe of all that you possess for me and desire to impart to me that I never even dreamed of.

In you, Jesus, I long to live, move, and have my being. May it be so, as I step out to trust you as the One who created and sustains my life. I am starting to delight in you. I will trust this womb-like place you have me in. I long to see your glory revealed, and my inner person revealed through your purposes, value, and identity. I want you more.

Submission

Acquiring a delight in Father's ways and life design enables us to live graciously in submission to Him in four distinct areas. Submission is required in all walks of life. As a lover of the One who loves you and keeps your best interests in mind, His structure and systems are worthy of our submission to authority.

Submission to Authority

Since the kidnapping in the garden, no one really likes authority. We have been born rebels from that point on. Although our sin nature has been ransomed, it is our choice to allow the application of submission to work. It is perhaps one of the most misunderstood aspects of God's heart and character. Submission in God's plan is freeing. Submission in man's plan is often legalistic, harsh, and is a haven for bondage.

Do you like to be told what to do? There are a handful of people that like to know what the rules are upfront in a given situation. Mostly, they like this because they don't want to break a rule, get caught, and then feel embarrassed. That's not true submission to authority. In order to deal with authority, we must first deal with submission that leads to freedom.

According to Charles Kraft: "The governing principle is, submission puts one under the authority of the one to whom we submit, and we get whatever the character of that one dictates."1 So if it is in our tender affection for Father that we find ourselves more deeply willing to submit to the One who holds the entire universe together, we will begin to obtain His character. What is His character? Love, kindness, certainty, truth, and freedom! Obtaining His character is glorious as we realize there are some things we don't want to be responsible for or have control over!

There are four types of authority we are called to submit to:

1. The ultimate authority God has over all His creation: gravity, seasons, how things work together in the universe (Psalm 93:1).

    One of the treasures we have in Father is His sovereignty over this universe; its beauty, practical purposes, and how it holds together. Most can gladly accept this God-ordained authority over creation! Accept there are some burdens that are not yours to bear. Aren't you glad you don't have authority over

---

1   Kraft, Charles. *I Give You Authority.*

gravity, the seasons, and how things collectively work in the universe?

When we try to exercise authority over God's system of how the universe works, we can soon find ourselves and the universe upside down. What God creates, He sustains. When He created life systems, it included a way to sustain them as long as He wants. We have a responsibility to God to care for and enjoy what He created.

But something is out of balance in our understanding of ultimate authority when we recycle paper out of fear of losing a tree, yet abort a baby and call it courage to do the right thing in uncomfortable situations. Based on how He set the life design to operate, can we not expect a core implosion with an imbalanced view of ultimate authority? When we put ourselves in position to make God-sized decisions that only God has the capacity to make and live with, we set ourselves up for a core meltdown, and I'm not just talking about the earth's core. I'm talking about the pearl's core. Hanging on to plastic and tossing our own flesh and blood is upside down.

2. The authority given to man over woman and family (1 Cor. 11:3, Heb. 13:17, 1 Tim. 3:4–12).

The feminist movement I talked about in the introduction of the book is what has destroyed this God-planned system of order and structure. As you read the above Scriptures in harmony with the Genesis account, God will reveal to you His original plan. And in this revelation, you will not discover yourself devalued or demoted as many feminists would say. "Equal" does not mean "same." It is grievous to watch women grovel and fight for equal *roles* and recognition to the male, when it is equal *value* they are actually seeking. They already have equal value in God's creation. But the roles and qualities of being female suffered a type of neutering2 in order to achieve the perception of equality. In the search for what they thought was equality by some measurement, more power and a higher salary came at the expense of their own lovely qualities of femininity. In their fight to be equal, they diminish their own uniqueness. You will find that you are the only one with your role, and in that there is tremendous value.

"I struggled with submission to my husband for eighteen years. I had that thread of feminism and entitlement running through portions of my disposition. It caused conflict in many areas, some of which we still suffer the long-term consequences of. Upon making a commitment to submit to God and His plan for submission in my marriage, I began to have less body aches, less entanglements and

---

2   Sandford, Paula. *Healing for a Woman's Emotions*

arguments, less drive to be right, and much more peace. The Lord taught me it was not my burden to try and have the last word, or be the one who is always right. When I disagree with Guy, I surrender it to God, because it is His responsibility to be instructed by the Lord, work it out with Him, and if things turn out badly, it is God's responsibility to deal with Guy. It's not really my business. His grace is sufficient to fill in for my human husband, just like He does for me in all my brokenness and gaping inadequacies. I have a lot more freedom in my life…and my marriage. I have more space for the presence of God and less space for the compulsive need to be right. The pain in marriage, like a parasite, is necessary to produce the pearls in your marriage. They are the treasures that can only be held close between you and your husband.

3. The civil authority in compatibility to God's commands (Rom. 13:1–6, 1 Pet. 2:13).

   When God began teaching me about authority and submission to Him as my creator and loving planner, I found myself in a submission to the order of the day; however, it began to unfold. In other words, instead of speeding and weaving in and out of cars to gain some sort of elusive control, I learned to keep the legal speed as I drive, and almost every time, I arrive on time or He rearranges time or traffic in the circumstances.

4. Personal authority in the spirit (Col. 1:13).

A Pearl Girl is given authority in her spirit to decide who and what will reign there. If I am fearful, I know that it says in 2 Timothy 1:7 that this spirit doesn't come from God. "I didn't give you a spirit of fear and timidity. But a spirit of love, power, and a sound mind." Based on the truth of God's Word, you have the authority to decide what and who rules you. You have the authority, and through intimacy with the Lord, to decide what reigns in your mind and will. As Christians, this is probably one of the most valuable parts of your inheritance for enduring the distance of the faith journey.

"Behold, I have given you authority to tread on serpents and scorpions, and over all the power of the enemy and nothing shall hurt you," (Luke 10:19). Our enemy, Satan, hates it when a Pearl Girl gets a strong core (soul and spirit), especially in the area of authority. He gets less access, less results when he baits her, and much less attention. Think about it, perhaps your mom, boyfriend, best friend, or spouse says something negative about you or someone else. You have the authority, in that moment, to buy into the negativity, to participate in the judgment of a person—or walk away from it. If you have experienced the love and presence of God then you know how God values the person being gossiped about. Or perhaps you were once the subject of gossip and judgment by others. You have authority because you know the origin and authority of love and grace. The Holy Spirit witnesses it in you so, in that moment, who are you going to give the power to in your thoughts, in your core? The voice of truth? You have been given spiritual authority through your intimate affection and connection with the Father. Use it! Stand up! That doesn't mean you go around rebuking people; it does mean you speak truth and we rebuke the enemy whenever necessary!

If you have lived with a lot of fear in your life, it takes time for the Holy Spirit to break down the hold it has on your thought life. It helped me to couple the principle of spiritual authority with spiritual permission! The Lord revealed to me that I actually have permission to *not* fear, fret, and worry. For someone like me who had lived many years feeling responsible for everyone's happiness or blame for unhappiness, hearing His voice say I have permission to rest released me from feeling the weight of responsibility and fretting over it.

You have authority imputed to you simply because you believed and accepted the saving power of Jesus. However, choosing to walk in the loving and intimate presence of your Heavenly Father repositions you to know things you didn't know before—like permission to *not* do something. You have permission not to worry. Not to fret. He releases you, through His loving presence, to rest in Him. You have permission to rest. You are not responsible *for* the scary, dark, bad things that Satan tries to trip you up with. You are responsible *to* rest and not fret. To trust and not fear.

Describe some areas of your life where respect for authority is strong and vibrant:

Is there someone(s) you have a difficult time agreeing with who are in a place of authority in your life? Parents, teachers, coach, pastor, or boss.

If you take the time to realize the burden of responsibility placed on them, are you more likely to gain more respect for their position?

In prayer, ask God to help you connect the importance of His divine authorities in your life with becoming a secure and joyful girl.

Lord Jesus,

I finally realize part of the reason I have felt burdened and discontent is...

Thank you Lord for having a blueprint for life. I am learning to love your planned design of how things work together in an orderly way that not only gives me peace, but pleases you. Help me to submit to the authority you have carefully and lovingly placed in my life.

I am loving being your daughter. Amen.

When you set your affections upon Him, you will be delivered. He lingers where He is loved, and deliverance will accompany Him. Psalm 91:14, "Because he (she) has set his (her) love upon me, I will deliver him (her)…. (She) shall call upon me and I will answer." Your authentic affection ushers Him into your life to be found, loved, and valued continuously.

What once was a lost and wandering parasite is becoming something lovely.

Endurance

Truth Concept

> My grace is sufficient for you, for my power is
> made perfect in weakness. Therefore I will boast
> all the more gladly of my weaknesses, so that
> the power of Christ may rest upon me.

> —2 Corinthians 12:9

Value Concept

I CAN ENDURE anything this life brings through knowing my value in the deep love and grace of Father.

Battle Cry

I can let God have His perfect purposes in my imperfect life.

Application

I can receive God's forgiveness and learn to love, respect, and forgive myself and others.

The Presence of Pain

A NATURAL PEARL forms inside an oyster when the shell has been *invaded by a parasite*. Tucked inside the womb of an oyster, the parasite accepts the painful process of surrendering to the nacre; the very substance that makes it One with it, and what eventually becomes a pearl. The power of the ocean, the rubbing irritants, the protective nacre, all work together to solidify the pearl. The pearl gets stronger and more beautiful over time. In the pearl industry, pricing and quality of the nacre's thickness determines the pearl's ability to last. So it is, with the nacre of God's love as you learn to endure in pain and suffering.

During painful seasons of life, a well-developed affection for the Father will give you the necessary grit for staying tucked in to Him while He accomplishes His purposes. If affection has not yet developed, the pain will drive you there. The pain always has a purpose—to deepen your affection, or give you one. He waits to be wanted. What once was a parasitic longing for *any* affection to fill your holes, has the capacity to become a beautiful intimacy between Father and daughter.

Like the pearl that rests in the womb of an oyster host, will you let Him bring His beautiful purposes to rest on you? Or will you fight and resist His painful purposes, turning your relationship with Him into a tomb of lifeless and powerless activity? Long for Him more as you surrender your heart to grow deeply tender toward the lover of your soul. Yes, He permits the pain, because He loves what its purpose is… and that's to produce the pearl of you that He saw before the foundations of the world. What pain are you enduring right now? A painful relationship with your mother? An unexpected illness? Are you a girl who has had a parasite in your life? Are you experiencing it because of poor choices or someone's invasion to your body or soul? What has been done that makes you feel as though you just walked into a dark, musty, empty tomb? What is sucking the life out of you?

Melody came to me at church one day asking if she could come for counseling. When she came for her first session, she told the story of how her life had been invaded by abuse. As she talked at her first appointment, I began to calculate the damage. It was impossible in human terms to even think that the damage could be accurately assessed, much less restored. I went home grieved more deeply over her story of pain than any I had ever heard.

Melody had been the childhood victim of a sexual/spiritual abuse parasite known as a church deacon. From the age of eleven, she suffered at the hands of a man who, like a parasite, grew, fed, and hid by eating up her very core from the inside out. She was ravaged, and the trip to my office was her first cry for help.

Despite the invasion to the oyster, a soothing substance known as nacre begins to coat and cover over the parasite because the oyster alone cannot expel the irritant. This process is known as encystation, which means to be enclosed in a cyst.

Melody carried an encystation. Her core had things that entered it that were parasitic and could offer nothing but pain. A pearl inside the oyster has a slimy, smooth, protecting substance called nacre. The nacre is constantly present in the pearl womb to offer protection until it is ready to be harvested as a full-term pearl.

God has been present with you since you were in your mother's womb. You have God's presence at every point of hurt, invasion, and encystation. His love and care from conception has watched over you. He has seen you and waits for you to see Him. He longs to be known in the pain to show you its purpose. All this works out according to your belief system and how agreeable you are with the truth of how and why you are here. That's why we discussed those things in previous chapters: shelter of love, reclaiming your inheritance, and affections that comprise your disposition.

A pearl becomes mature and beautiful through endurance. Father God permits the pain, resistance, and irritation so you can, like the pearl enduring its painful development, be brought out to show your God-given identity and beauty—ultimately revealing God's glory. God receives glory when you live and move and be in His intended design. Who He says you are is your true identity and intended to be a direct reflection of Him. You are not your issues.

I heard the testimony of a sex trafficking victim I will call Joyce. She was kidnapped and held in captivity for several years. While in captivity, she was forced to have sex with her captor, cook for him, and was never free to walk out—often kept in a locked room, or even chained to a piece of furniture. One day, a neighbor came over while her captor was gone. She had the courage to scream that day and the neighbor came in and freed her. She was weak, broken, injured, and had lost all her sense of value. The only identity she had was the ability to remember her name. Her mind had been marinated in lies through all her captor's demands and violations. Shame and pain permeated her entire being and so believed she deserved everything that happened to her.

After her rescue and being cared for by people who facilitate the recovery of human trafficking victims, much prayer, assistance, and intensive counseling helped her mind to heal. She became able to hear truth, believe it, and activate it in her decisions and will. Her emotions stabilized through truth. By the time I heard her speak, she had been freed for about a year. She radiated the love of Christ. Standing before a live audience in a city auditorium at a human trafficking awareness event, she testified to the deep love of God. She had already forgiven her captor.

She had been broken, completely void of God's felt love, battered and torn—reflecting all that the enemy had warred against her. Now, recovered by truth and love of God, her identifier and value giver, she stood reflecting Him, not the enemy. She had a glow and a confidence that had been identified and reclaimed as her own. The invisible crown jewels in her heart shone through her eyes, authoritative voice, confidence, and courage. She had even come so far she wanted to give back and help others who had lost their identity and value through the shameless acts of abuse, usury, and violence. Unspeakable pain had become spoken love and visible glory.

There are two sources of pain: the pain of people and the pain of life. God always has lovely outcomes in mind for pain. He doesn't waste anything that comes into our life. One aspect of people pain often comes from the tongue. What God intended to be a source of truth, affirmation, and praise is a deep source of pain for so many.

Pain of Words that Attack Your Value

HAVE YOU EVER stopped and asked yourself where the poisonous remarks originated? Hurt people, hurt others.

> And the tongue is a fire, a world of wickedness set among our members, contaminating and depraving the whole body and setting on fire the wheel of birth (the cycle of man's nature), being itself ignited by hell. For every kind of beast and bird, of reptile and sea animal, can be tamed and has been tamed by human genius. But the human tongue can be tamed by no man. It is a restless (undisciplined, irreconcilable) evil, full of deadly poison. With it we bless the Lord and Father, and with it we curse men who were made in God's likeness! (James 3:6–9, AMP).

You may not stop and ask yourself that question because you're so busy licking your wounds and trying to figure out how to survive in the moment. If you can remember the fact that hurt people hurt others, it will serve you well to not take things so seriously in some situations.

When my husband was pastoring, an older gentleman abruptly approached my fifteen-year-old son during the Sunday morning service. Greyson was sitting on the front row when the man approached with hurtful words and yelled, "Take your hat off in chuuurch!"

This humiliated my son, and even though it doesn't seem like a big deal to the man who inflicted with words, my son took it very seriously. The confusion and shame this caused Greyson could have been prevented had the elderly gentleman handled his opinions differently. Greyson was already highly aware of unruly curly hair as a young teenager. Putting a hat on damp hair helped him gain a sense of personal mastery over caring for his hair and looking presentable. But for whatever reason, this man felt hurt or disrespected in some way. If he had approached Guy and I, it could have been handled totally different. His words hurt not only Greyson, but Guy and I as well. We were left asking the question, "Does he think Greyson is an orphan and that we don't parent him?" If we felt it was important for Greyson to remove his hat, we certainly would have told him so. Words can hurt everyone they come into contact with.

When you find yourself on the receiving end of a verbal accusation and/or attack, apply these truths:

Remember the truth and recognize where the words come from. Much of our wrestling in this life is due to the spiritual battle between the forces. Forces we cannot see as visual entities, but most definitely see their activity. When people war against each other with debilitating put-downs, sarcasm, and words, Paul instructs us to remember this, "For we do not wrestle against flesh and blood, but against the rulers, against the authorities, against the cosmic powers over this present darkness, against the spiritual forces of evil in the heavenly places." David also spoke about the tongue being used for evil in Psalm 52:2 when he said, "Your tongue devises destruction. Like a sharp razor, working deceitfully."

When someone attacks your value, it is really important to stop the message from getting into your belief system. It may not be possible to stop your verbal attacker, but the enemy is on the prowl seeking out a tasty emotional meltdown and you must see it as an attack and handle as such starting on the inside of you. You belong to the Father, and the enemy is not really allowed to touch your inner core, but he can make you think he can.

Run to your Heavenly Father, your shelter of love, first. Remember, no one can separate you from the Father's love—your innermost personal shelter and strong tower.

I hear people call each other names—and not by their given names. I see the effects of those vile words and put-downs in the counseling room every day. When someone calls you a name or describes you in vile terms, you are put in a position to stand tall or shrink back. By standing tall, I am not referring to a self-defense debate or a physical fight. Stand tall on the inside knowing that the God of the universe delights in you and someone else's words do not change or alter who you are or your value. They may hurt your feelings, but feelings don't give you your value. Neither does someone else's pain that gets spewed all over you. Truth does. Stand up on the inside knowing your true value as a person has not been diminished. Run home to that hiding place in the Father's love where you encounter His presence and are always received, delighted in, and accepted.

Pay attention to the words in parenthesis as I place emphasis on how the truth of God's heart in the verse can *apply* to a verbal attack. I placed emphasis on what the Holy Spirit's voice *might be* trying to interject into your ear as you digest and meditate on His word.

> For this reason (Yes, I heard what he/she said) I bow my knees to the Father of our Lord Jesus Christ, from whom the whole family in heaven and earth is named, that He would grant you, according to the riches of His glory, (remember I have crowned you with jewels of love, redemption, and loving kindness,) to be strengthened with might through His Spirit, in the inner man, (the enemy and his lies cannot touch your inner man. I am in the most secret place in you where I speak to you and love you and pour out value on you) that Christ may dwell (I see you and stay with

you in the hurt place in your hearts) through faith (agree with me and believe the truth of what I tell you); that you being rooted and grounded in love, (I am your Home. I am eternal. Return to me as your life source. I am present. I am love,) may be able to comprehend with all the saints (there are others. You are not alone—but I see you) what is the width and length and depth and height (My love goes deeper than the shame spewed from the worst accusation or name-calling) to know the love of Christ (He is my precious son who loved me through incomprehensible burden and pain) which passes knowledge; and that you may be filled with all the fullness of God. (I am a perpetual life-giving source that never runs out. I am willing to fill you with as much as you want of me). (Eph. 3:14–19)

Renew truth in your mind

Begin to meditate on the meaning of the Lord's instruction in Romans 12:2. Let it get into your soul: "'Do not be conformed to this world, but be transformed by the renewing of your mind, that you may prove what is that good and acceptable and perfect will of God.' 'Okay,' you say, 'but what does that mean?'"

Conformed: What does the world tell you to do when you are treated unjustly? Get retaliation. Any human retaliation you come up with is wimpy. His justice is exacting, piercing, and just. (Deuteronomy 32:4: "He is the Rock. His work is perfect; for all His ways are justice, A God of truth and without injustice; Righteous and upright is He.") So let Him pick up that nasty word attack and deal effectively and eternally with it.

Transformed: Go into transforming mode. Pull out all the spiritual weaponry you have to defeat the true enemy, which really isn't that person who just treated you unfairly. It is the enemy—Satan. (1 Peter 5:8: "Be sober, be vigilant; because your adversary the devil walks about like a roaring lion, seeking whom he may devour.") A girl who surrenders herself to a just God will be transformed. You will know it too. His Spirit won't hide it from you.

Renew your mind: In that defining moment of attack or disrespect, you have two options: One is to give their words of attack—their voice—a higher place of value than the truth about who God says you are. The second is to worship God and His truth above all. *Believe the truth concerning His view of you instead of the lie.* In our sin nature, it's just easier to believe the lie. That's why it's considered a battle. It's not against just flesh and blood, it's against principalities that are at work to give you false comfort and keep you in what you've always known. It is painful to change to something new.

I was recently told the story of a toddler who had spent most of her life in a car seat. She was fed, diapered, kept there, and slept there. Eventually, she was placed in a loving home. When her new love-filled caregiver would lift the child out the car seat and put her down to crawl or sleep, the child screamed in pain for weeks because her little body had conformed to the car seat. Conforming to truth is worth the pain and the inner fight.

Ephesians 6:12 says, "For we do not wrestle against flesh and blood, but against principalities, against powers, against the rulers of the darkness of this age, against spiritual hosts of wickedness in the heavenly places."

Prove: The flesh can't prove anything spiritual. Our flesh and self-effort will only prove that, in the world, someone will always be smarter, prettier, or better at sarcasm or rock throwing. His Spirit, however, if given a chance in your will, proves He does have a better plan and that He will accomplish it in you. (Romans 8:28: "And we know that all things work together for good to those who love God, to those who are called according to His purpose.") There it is again, He takes delight in the plan and purpose of your existence and He can prove it!

Perfect will: He is in control of all outcomes. It's just a matter of whether we believe it or not. What seems negative in the earthly realm, He will work out in the heavenly realm. (2 Corinthians 12:9: "My grace is sufficient for you, for my strength is made perfect in weakness. Therefore most gladly I will rather boast in my infirmities that the power of Christ may rest on me.")

Let it go! Walk out of the trap set for you!

The phrase "let it go" implies that something is trying to hang on. Whatever it is—whether it is a lie, an offense, or looking at an invitation to a pity party—you don't have time to analyze. Let it go before it gets a stronger grasp. Satan will throw images and lies at you until one sticks. Don't let it stick. Let it go. Submit it to God in your will, then *the power of God will rest on you* to walk out the trap. But if you try to figure out what happened before you let it go, the trap will snap and you will be caught. Being paralyzed by fear is exactly where the enemy wants us. Then it requires a small battalion to get you out. Walking out the trap before it is set increases your strength and endurance. Getting trapped over and over will wear down your ability to endure.

If you've ever seen an actual mousetrap, then you can understand this concept. In order for the mouse to be caught, it has to be baited. Usually the mouse hunter will put some peanut butter or a tiny piece of cheese on the trap. This draws the mouse in for a good smell and snoop. As the mouse takes the time to analyze the situation and decide if he wants to eat it, the metal arm is released, and his head or his tail is caught under it. Sometimes they wiggle their way out, but often they will stay there until they are found by their mouse trapper. Then it's over. The mouse is often dead by the time the trapper finds it. It's the same way with verbal attacks. They come through humans, but are motivated and inspired by Satan. Once he realizes he can bait you, he will make someone his messenger to say awful things. Sometimes this is a family member or even a parent. Regardless, if you take the bait and begin believing those words are for you to eat, then you will be trapped in an emotional storm that requires a lot of help to get out of. You must act quickly when verbal attacks come. If you seek out other people and tell them what happened and how much it hurts over and over with hopes that they will side with you, then the trap has been set for you to be pulled into emotional quicksand. Hurt leads to gossiping and backbiting. Before you know it, relationship dynamics have turned toxic, deceitful, and relationships are destroyed.

First, it comes as bait, then an offense, then a trap with seemingly no way out. Mean girl cliques and bullies are comprised of such dynamics. Choose to believe the truth about who and what your heavenly Father says you are. Recognize the source of the attack, and run away from it and into the arms of your Heavenly Father where unconditional love will meet you. His love is the shelter where protection and clarity reside over verbal attacks.

Pain from Words that Attack Your Existence

HURTING WORDS STING and make you question your value. But abusive words have a pointed arrow that rips and tears at the soul. When they fall on you, it can make you question the validity of your very existence.

> "You are fat and lazy!"
> "Why are you so stupid?"
> "I thought you were smarter than that!"
> "You are an idiot."
> "You are useless. You are replaceable."
> "You are an embarrassment."
> "You are nothing."
> "I'm going to kill you if…"
> "You're nothing but a worthless piece of s——t!"
> "You were supposed to be a boy!"

The oyster alone cannot expel the irritant. Likewise, you alone cannot get rid of shame. There is not enough good deeds in the world you can do to remove shame. When you offered your heart to Christ, He declared your debt was paid, but the pain of shame requires time for healing. You may be in the right standing with God, but it takes time to walk out on the earth what is already true in heaven. You are meant to be here. God delights in your existence. He has a plan for loveliness, and a purpose for you to fulfill. You are allowed to stay. Jesus, the breath of heaven declares it.

Five gallons of water filtering through an oyster per day washes, cleans, feeds, soothes, and touches the parasite. It doesn't remove it. The living water of Jesus filters through your heart washing, loving, cleaning, feeding, soothing, and healing your very existence. It takes eight to twenty years for a pearl to form. It takes time for the pain to finish its perfect work. "Consider it a sheer gift, friends, when tests and challenges come at you from all sides. You know that under pressure, your faith-life is forced into the open and shows its true colors. So don't try to get out of anything prematurely. Let it do its work so you become mature and well-developed, not deficient in any way" (James 1:2–4, MSG).

Can I say it another way?

You are in the presence of relentless love when you experience hurt, trials, and challenges. This love monitors the pressure in such a way that you will be a finished and shimmering beauty in due time. So please don't take a shortcut. Please don't make any quick and sudden moves out of discomfort. Let this relentless plan for sacred beauty unfold at the perfect time. Stay, please stay, until His glory shows.

I have a sign in my office that says, "The way out of pain is through it." A willingness to walk through pain with Jesus is the way of healing. We don't heal from words, abuse, betrayal, and other kinds of parasites apart from walking through it. In Luke 9:23, Jesus taught that if any man (or woman) would be His disciple, he would need to deny himself, take up his cross every day, and follow him. Thus, the sign in my office. Sometimes girls arrive at a very painful intersection in their life and in order to deal with it they:

Run
Cover
Stay

Some feel the pain of an unfaithful boyfriend and run into the arms of a new one. Or just run. Some feel the pain of an unfaithful husband and cover for him, excusing his behavior, and neglecting their own value.

Some experience pain through horrific neglect and abuse. Some feel the pain of loss, but with the truth of their value and the unconditional love of God, choose to stay in Him throughout the course of the pain with the sole purpose of learning from it. They find healing in staying in the shadow of the cross until His glory is revealed.

The key word in Luke 9:23 is "deny." The cross diagram illustrates how we are meant to stay at the intersection of pain and powerlessness. It's in the staying and admitting our powerlessness in the pain and circumstances that God's power is able to release through our surrender and be glorified. Then we are released from pain. But only because we offered ourselves to God in the midst of it, grieved the losses, and surrendered.

> Doing life is the vertical line where you are simply living your life and everything seems fine, but then…

> Enters surprises and suffering at the horizontal line where an unexpected surprise or a type of suffering enters your life (see Luke 9:23)

> Not in control is the large dot in the intersection on the cross where you have to make a choice to stay and admit your weakness, run away from the pain, or dance around it in denial. (See 2 Corinthians 12:9a)

> Yield and surrender is the dotted line representing His power and glory rising up in you when you made the choice to stay, admit your weakness, and die to all your own human ability to survive. You choose to trust Him. (See 2 Corinthians 12:9b)

YIELDING MAKES A WAY FOR HIS GLORY

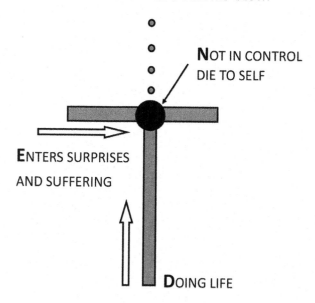

NOT IN CONTROL
DIE TO SELF

ENTERS SURPRISES
AND SUFFERING

DOING LIFE

Deny the use of your own tools of isolation, self-medicating, fighting, rebelling, running, and hiding when you are in a place of pain. Stay in it until God shows up. He will.

The Pain of Betrayal

HURTING WORDS AND verbal abuse certainly can betray the heart, but in this section, I am talking about the kind of radical betrayal that calls for radical forgiveness. The kind of forgiveness that looks offensive.

It isn't necessary to go into all the varying levels and types of betrayals. We have all experienced betrayal at some point in our life. But for our purposes here, it's most important to note that all betrayal comes in through the area of trust. We don't feel betrayed unless we first trusted the betrayer. So in order to deal with betrayal, we must first look at trust.

Think of the relationships you have in your life that are founded on the capacity and desire for trust: spouse, best girlfriend, parents, youth pastor, boyfriend, teacher, coach, mentor, and roomie. As you grow through the seasons of your womanhood, you have your spouse, your boss, your neighbor, and your children. Wherever there is relationship, there is potential for betrayal. The felt depth of the betrayal is often in direct correlation with the depth of trust. Unless God, the shelter of love and source of truth, is at the center of how you view these relationships, betrayal will be extremely difficult and sometimes impossible to overcome.

Betrayal doesn't just hit us like an irritant. It hits us like a boulder between the eyes and then sits, often lingering on top of our heart for years. It can be crushing. If someone pried open the oyster shell and messed with the protecting nacre or pulled the pearl out before it was finished forming, it would halt the development. Without intervention, the pearl may be poorly formed. So it is with betrayal in the pearl girl. Betrayal is the old bait-and-switch routine. Exactly like what Satan did in the garden. He baited Eve, softened her up, and then snap went the trap. Have you ever experienced bait and switch from someone you trusted? Felt like your heart was ripped out? God sees. Your Heavenly Father sees your pain of being betrayed.

This injury of betrayal needs attention. If left unattended, it festers anger and plants deep roots of resentment and an inability to trust even when it's safe.

I would like to address three forms of betrayal:

> Family (those closest to us)
> Others (acquaintances, strangers, etc.)
> Self

Family

You have read my story in the introduction. Mother leaving was a betrayal. Dad refusing to acknowledge my presence was a betrayal.

When God designed us to grow and develop, He planned it to happen in stages and in a family design. Luke 2:52 says that even "Jesus grew in wisdom, stature, and in favor with God and man." Basically that was referring to mental, physical, spiritual, and emotional growth. At each stage of development, we have varying capacities for trust based on our experience within the context of God's family design.

If a baby cries when it is hungry and it gets fed, it learns to trust in a source greater than they are. Of course, they can't form that concept or the words, but the trust muscles in their soul and spirit are working in symphony with how God designed them physically at that stage.

However, if a baby cries when it is hungry and does not get fed, that great symphony is inhibited. It is slow to develop the trust mechanism God designed to be growing at that point.

A seed of betrayal is planted in that child's heart that at some point must be dealt with. Unfortunately, that seed will grow as each stage of development arrives and involves more people and more potential for betrayal.

If you are reading this book and you have been betrayed by someone in your family or stepfamily, or family friend, there is a remedy. But please understand the remedy only works as you apply it. If you have been physically, sexually, verbally, or emotionally abused in any way by a family member, please know it is not an easy fix. In no way is this section intended to minimize what happened to you. It was evil. Jesus was and is deeply grieved by it and waits for you to turn to Him as the only remedy for the ripping caused by betrayal.

Others

Cheat. When others betray us it usually means they were trying to beat or cheat some system of beliefs or behaviors. Best friends cheat on us by telling our secrets. Boyfriends cheat on us when they start liking someone else. The spoken belief system is that best friends don't tell. Boyfriends don't kiss other girls. Ah, but they do. We feel cheated, betrayed.

The problem lies in the belief system. Once again, we are confronted with the fact that Satan, the enemy of our faith, is the father of lies. The remedy, at least in part, lies in who and what are we going to believe.

Self

How many times have you vowed to change something in your life? Maybe it is your behavior, your attitude, your grades, your scores, your skills. But you don't. You won't go back to that cheating boyfriend. You promise yourself you will try harder, work harder, be more, and just suck it up and do it. But you betray your own significance when you do. Again, there is a remedy. The remedy for betrayal is found in the same place it was birthed from. Trust.

Trust the depth.

In all the situations you can think of where you have been betrayed, there is a power that goes like a spade into the soil of your heart to get underneath that hurt and unearth it, bringing it up to the surface for validation, acknowledgment, and fresh air. Father's shelter of love (home base) and Jesus's personal betrayal and perfect work on the cross carries the power to surgically bring the hurt out to remove bitterness, anger, and unforgiveness. The remedy: trust His writhing work of forgiveness on the cross. The depth of the pain, both His and yours, serves to pronounce His love and grace go deeper still. You say, "But you don't know what he did to me." He does. You say, "But it was unforgivable! It would be wrong to forgive such an injustice!" He did. You say, "But I just can't stop thinking about how wrong it was! And I see this person every day."

He knows.

So if the worst sin you ever committed (which at this point may be unforgiveness) isn't too big for God to forgive, what makes you think you are better than the one who betrayed you?

Your personal betrayal may be crushing. There was another crushing I would like to tell you about: the crushing betrayal of Jesus by those closest to Him.

"Still, it's what God had in mind all along, to crush him with pain. The plan was that he give himself as an offering for sin so that he'd see life come from it–life, life, and more life. And God's plan will deeply prosper through him" (Isa. 53:10, MSG).

An Extravagant Price

THE LATIN ROOT word for excruciating is *cruciare* which means "to crucify." To inflict intense pain. To subject to intense mental distress.

After being beaten with a whip that literally tore His flesh each time the Romans slung it over and back, Jesus was asked to carry a heavy cross uphill while being cursed, spit on, and mocked. The blood mixed with sweat must have blinded His eyes from seeing His own steps. The thirst must have been unbearable.

Once arrived at the crucifixion sight, they used rough spikes that look a lot like today's railroad spikes. Thick and long. Picture a spike nearly the height of this book being hammered into the nerve centers of each hand.

The shame in crucifixion is revolting. Imagine being stripped to your underwear and being dragged to your nearest lookout point and hung up for everyone to see. Imagine the humility of your body mostly naked, dying in front of people that you know and even had meaningful encounters with.

I can't find words to describe what it must have been like for Jesus to experience the cruciare pain and humility while knowing His Father wasn't going to come get him.

> He stayed.
> He died.
> God's beauty and glory came.
> Eventually.

So was that good enough for you? Or is pride so great that even His horrific death isn't enough to cover the injustice done to you?

The weight of the world's sin wasn't just a boulder on the heart of Jesus. It was a boulder as big as the universe, because it covered every person in the universe from the beginning of time to the end. Do you know how many rapes that is? Do you know how many molestations and verbal attacks that is? And murder? The weight of all sin without the rescue of His Father suffocated Him.

> Stay in His presence long enough
> For Compassion to come
> Because He will.
> Forgive. Release. Walk without weight.

The most humbling experience is being forgiven.

The most freeing experience is to forgive.

"A man's (or girl's) pride will bring (her) low, but the humble in spirit will retain honor" (Prov. 29:23, AMP). "For if you forgive people their trespasses (their reckless and willful sins, leaving them, letting them go, and give up resentment), your heavenly Father will also forgive you" (Matt. 6:14, AMP).

A Holy God cannot stand the sight of the betrayal and evil performed against you. They both demand His wrath be released. But God's wrath was poured out on Jesus instead of you. Instead of me. Instead of *them*. Jesus was without sin; the perfect lamb sacrificed so God's wrath could be satisfied—and you, I, and they could live in peace with a Holy God and with each other. His satisfied wrath released their guilt.

Yes, it's true they may not have repented or accepted that truth yet, but perhaps you are still the one walking around with a boulder on your chest. Spiritually speaking, the boulder is actually on them until they do. Discipline yourself to believe that truth. Holding them to your own system of wrath and punishment simply postpones your own peace and freedom.

Satisfied wrath comes from the heart of God, and it's that same heart that pours out deep and satisfying love. Whatever horrors happen, His wrath was satisfied so that love could go deeper still. So let it.

Sometimes it is hardest to forgive ourselves. The wrath poured out on self often houses the deepest pain.

In 1979, I aborted a baby son. Several years later when I realized I had not cleaned out *tissue*, as the medical field referred to it, and that I had actually killed my baby, I named him Sully Patrick. There it is. I have said it a million times either to relieve someone else of their pain or to inflict pain on myself. But it has never been in print for someone else to pick up and read. The fact that it is now written down in a book tells me that I am secure in God's forgiveness as well as my own.

Perhaps you just filled up with judgment and decided to put this book down. Trust me, I understand. I not only judged myself, but I loathed myself until I encountered the abundant grace of the ultimate judge, Father God. Encountering His grace meant I had to endure facing a Holy God. Until I understood the depth of my sin in the presence of a holy and loving God, I couldn't even recognize the extravagant grace being extended.

The concept *about* God's forgiveness through the cross event had to move from an intellectual understanding to a personal encounter *with* Him. When I finally wanted Jesus more than forgiveness, He came to me carrying forgiveness in His arms. This encounter became my testimony of knowing Jesus, who willingly endured the wrath aimed at me. At the point, I wanted the forgiver more than the forgiveness. Father God began exposing His heart and tender voice to me. Knowing His forgiveness helped me experience permission to let myself off the hook of guilt and self-condemnation. He further helped me to see that I can walk out on the earth what is already true in heaven. I am forgiven. His work on the cross was deeper than the horror of abortion. His grace is sufficient. I will see Sully in heaven. There is no more condemnation because Christ's work was more powerful than any law. The law is only as strong as the flesh, and what I couldn't do for myself, Christ's work on the cross did completely. (Romans 8:1–3)

The closely kept secret had to get out of me many years ago. It ate at me, gnawed on my heart like a parasite in search of a place to rest. I knew in my theology that God had forgiven me, but the concept alone could not expel the parasite of guilt. The first person I ever told was my friend Sunni. Her grace and unconditional love without judgment positioned me to begin my personal healing journey. Telling someone enabled His love to begin sending gracious messages through her. It said, "This is devastating, yes, but not too devastating for me. I have always loved you, but I delight in your coming clean. You are still valuable to me."

My journey of healing took close to twenty years. They say it takes eight to twenty years for the parasite in the oyster to become a pearl, but I have friends who didn't take that long, and others who took longer. The point is, God has a purpose. Not only is His purpose perfect, but also is His timing. He delights in these and loves us while we are being formed in love, grace, and compassion. As He began to walk me through the healing process, He gently showed me the pride, fleshly lusts, selfishness, vulnerability to lies, and rebellion that ultimately led me to that clinic in the spring of 1979. And as deep as the evil and horror of baby holocaust goes, His love and grace go deeper still.

He forgave me. Jesus took the wrath from His own holy and loving Father for me. It is an insult to Him when parasitic guilt insists His substitution can't cover it. "Oh, so go do it again, Jesus, until I think you've done enough." That's even worse than baby holocaust! To believe the perfect little lamb wasn't beautiful enough! What evil pride! To think my sin is so great that even Jesus isn't beautiful and obedient enough to take my wrath. He had the idea of me, delighted in the idea, and saw fit for me to be born, and has a purpose and a passion for my existence. Still.

Yes, I suit up every day in my shelter of love and reclaim my inheritance to walk in the freedom He gave me...even though I reached in and snuffed the earthly existence of Sully Patrick. Yes, I suit up every day in my shelter of love and reclaim my inheritance to walk in the freedom He gave me... even though I stopped the idea and delight of Sully all those years ago.

So how can I deserve to be delighted in? You're exactly right, I don't deserve it. But His grace covers the undeserving heart. His love permeates the exact effect of your sin and mine. Grace is so radical, it can be offensive. He knew. Before the foundation of the world. When I became His idea, He knew. And He still brought me here. He waited to be wanted by me, and relates to me in forgiveness—not condemnation.

God had the idea of Sully too. When Sully was His idea, He delighted in it. He knew I would stand at that crossroad and choose to snuff out his life. I lost out. Sully lost out because he never got to take an earthly breath or exercise his choices.

In the healing process, I came to learn the one central factor in not only the decision to end Sully's life, but also the behaviors that landed me there: I couldn't trust myself. My inner core was not established. I didn't know who I was, and I certainly didn't know my value from God's perspective. Getting pregnant out of wedlock and not being able to trust me, the baby's father, or anyone else led me and my baby to the slaughterhouse (a physical slaughter for Sully, an emotional one for me)...an abortion clinic. I was terribly insecure on the inside. All my false senses of security were based on what I looked like, how well I could perform and please people, expectations of success, my image, and managing the pain I didn't even know I was carrying from the age of five. I referenced so many outside sources to manage my life that I didn't even know who I was. Why on earth would I attempt to trust a medical staff I had never met more than I could trust myself to be a mother? Or trust the opinion of a university professor more than I could trust myself to be a mommy? His response to my uncontrollable weeping in class was to "get myself on a bus and go get it taken care of." As though I needed a tooth pulled. Only the enemy can package lies like that one.

Through counseling, a postabortion support group, journaling, soul searching, and Bible study, God graciously led me to the root of this horrific betrayal one spring afternoon.

Abandoned women abandon others—even helpless babies. One spring afternoon, I agreed to meet with Jesus in a chair at my home where my other two children had grown up. In this agreement with myself, Jesus, and my postabortion group, I was to keep my heart open to whatever He wanted to show me regarding the loss of that precious baby. I was asking Him for complete healing, closure, and fearless intimacy in His pure presence!

A few minutes into the conversation, He gave me a picture of meeting Sully in heaven. In God's loving presence, the grief surfaced; it came like self-inflicting pain at first, but like the parasite, I knew there was no place to go. I chose to stay there in that moment, turned inside out, until I could receive what the Lord was wanting to bring. After waiting for what seemed like a few minutes, love flooded into me as I cast the eyes of my soul on my precious son, Sully Patrick. The Lord showed His favor in this tender moment, and I was able to express maternal words toward my son. It was in the pain of this that I actually felt maternal toward this child for the first time. From that God-designed maternal place in my heart, I was released from the shame of abortion. It left me. Love took its place. I encountered forgiveness, and though it was with deep grief, I released Sully fully into the care of Jesus. We all agreed the account was settled on my behalf and that we will meet again when I get there. The concept of forgiveness alone could not expel the parasite, but the power and presence of God did.

Jesus was there in that *surgery* room to receive baby Sully. Jesus was deeply grieved but lovingly waited to be needed and wanted. He knew the pain of this parasitic event would need His love in order for me to turn to Him as my remedy for guilt, mistrust, and self- condemnation.

God forgave me. Jesus enabled it. Sully agreed to it. I had to make a decision. Would I agree to it too? Would I be willing to receive the remedy?

Forgiveness is the remedy for endurance in this life. We need His forgiveness and we must offer it. Even to ourselves. Yes, God had the idea of me, delighted in the idea, and saw fit for me to be born and has a purpose and a passion for my existence.

Now, knowing what I know, aborting the very idea and earthly existence of Sully Patrick deeply grieved the heart of God. When I ended his entire earthly life, it must have brought unspeakable disdain to God. Jesus satisfied His disdain through the cross, and now God's love and grace go deeper still. Sully Patrick lives. He is in heaven. God's love and grace go deeper still. I live and count my every breath in gratitude to Jesus for His perfect work on the cross to cover my sin against God, Sully, his father, and myself.

The cross is the gateway. Forgiveness on the cross is the remedy.

Sully's father did not want the abortion. It hurt him greatly when I made the decision against his will. A short time before the encounter in my chair at home, I wrote to him and asked him for forgiveness. *Will you forgive me* are four very powerful words. Forgiving conversations occurred between Jesus and everyone around Him the day He was crucified. The thief humbled himself asking Jesus to please remember him that day in paradise. He had a revelation of forgiveness watching a perfect man die a humiliating and undeserving death. He watched Jesus cry out from the cross, "Father forgive them for they know not what they do."

At the intersection on the cross, we find that endurance, staying put through imperfection and weakness instead of running, makes a way for God's perfect power and strength to rise up instead. Endurance, even in pain, forges a way for His glory to be seen. Especially in the dark places. [See p. 137.]

After reviewing my letter, Sully's father wrote back and said, "I forgave you a long time ago." Forgiveness is our most enduring weapon against the enemy because Satan hates it when we discover true forgiveness. It produces love and splashes grace everywhere.

Endurance. There are so many ways we can get taken out from the race. But 2 Timothy 4:7 implies there is victory: "I have fought the good fight, I have finished the race, and I have kept the faith." His forgiveness is sufficient and serves to be the endurance we need for life. "Therefore He is able also to save to the uttermost (completely, perfectly, finally, and for all time and eternity) those who come to God through Him, since He is always living to make petition to God and intercede with Him and intervene for them. Here is the

High Priest (perfectly adapted) to our needs, as was fitting-holy, blameless, unstained by sin, separated from sinners, and exalted higher than the heavens" (Heb. 7:25–26, AMP; emphasis mine).

A pearled life learns to endure anything this life brings her way by knowing her value and the love of a pure and holy God who forgives.

Like the pearl tucked inside the oyster, please press into the womb of His presence where you can experience Him, not just a concept. Encounter love, respect, and forgiveness for your own self and others. His love, grace, and forgiveness go deeper than any hurt or betrayal.

Watchful: Get your God-designer glasses on for seeing both near and far. Put them on and only take them off for sleeping. While you are sleeping, your Father will be diligent to watch over you that you might find rest. His job is to never rest.

You can be certain that Satan hates it when you finally understand how beautiful and valuable you are. Upon gaining this pearl, he will be after it. At the same time, he ups his game, you must up yours. Be watchful to recognize the people, places, and things he tries to work through to steal this new possession.

At the same time, be watchful of all the ways Father's presence protects, leads, strengthens, and empowers you.

Prowl: Get your Jesus camo on. This will keep you tucked in close to Him where it makes it more difficult for the enemy to spot you or dare to come near. The enemy is on the prowl. You can know that God and Satan operate completely different. "God works with integrity. Satan works with deception. God leads His followers to freedom. Satan leads his to captivity."[1] Learn to sense the difference.

Devour: Be sure to put on your perfume as you walk in your truth suit. You get what you attract. Anything that stinks up your suit in the way of impure sensuality will stimulate the nostrils of the enemy and his spirit cronies. If there is a holy fragrance present, the craving for something to devour

1   Kraft, Charles. *The Rules of Engagement*

diminishes. The cravings of deceit, bitterness, lust, power, manipulation, and self will shrink. Give him nothing to crave.

Resist: Put on your fiery dart-proof vest. The enemy will try to shoot when he can't get close. But what he shoots are fiery darts, relying on the element of surprise, especially in your weak or restful moments. There are no vacations. You can go on vacation away from work, friends, family, but you cannot vacation from the battle. He especially shoots arrows when we are sick. The dart-proof vest covers your heart and protects your core from being penetrated. If he can get to the core, he's able to attack your identity and take you down. But remember, he can't have your core. He can only make you think he has it. You belong to the king. You are meant to be. But Satan likes you to think that even though those are the facts, your daughterhood is powerless.

Firm: A firm and right stance at all times will protect you from being knocked to the ground. A girl ready for battle has her feet in a firm stance in the Word of God, and her heart set upon Him as her highest affection. This makes her immovable, no matter how difficult the attack may be. God's written as well as spoken word over her will keep her firm in her belief of truth. She knows the depth, height, breadth, and width of His love.

Suffering: The microfiber cloth in the left pocket of your shrink suit will help keep your suit polished when you weep from hurt and suffering. The salt in the tears will be a great abrasive to make your suit shine. A girl who is suited for battle knows she will hurt and suffer. It's not how much or how little she suffers, but how well she embraces its purpose to bring glory, much like the glory of a shining armor. A pearl girl lives her shimmer!

In a little while: The beautiful watch with the pearl in the center keeps time in eternity. If you want to know earthly time, you will need to get a different watch. If you want to know eternal time, this watch will help you see how quickly your trials come and go. Gratefulness helps pass the earthly hours. A pearl girl trusts her Father's timing.

Grace: You'll notice a plastic card resembling a credit card in the rear pocket of your truth suit. It is linked to the heart of God and will always show a grace balance in your favor. In this accounting system, there will always be what you need.

And establish you: Dressing for battle by your own free choice every day will serve to establish *you*. At the end of your life and when your earthly battle is done, you will look back and see how all this served to establish you in your core. It establishes your value because, with each battle fought and won, you can understand the extravagant cost that Jesus paid for you in His ultimate battle on the cross.

In Hebrews 12:1–3, the writer teaches us to look to Jesus as our example of endurance: "Therefore, since we are surrounded by so great a cloud of witnesses, let us also lay aside every weight, and sin which clings so closely, and let us run with endurance the race that is set before us, looking to Jesus, the founder and perfector of our faith, who for the joy that was set before him endured the cross, despising the shame, and is seated at the right hand of the throne of God. Consider him who endured from sinners such hostility against himself, so that you may not grow weary or fainthearted."

Pure

Biblical Truth

> Draw near to God, and He will draw near to you.
> Cleanse your hands...purify your hearts...
>
> —James 4:8

Value Concept

I am valued by a pure and holy God and this value determines what I value.

Battle Cry

My heart is purified by the infusion of God's holiness, grace, and love; it is not performance driven, but desires purity.

Application

I am what I contain.

Pure Infusion

THERE IS NOTHING we can do to make ourselves pure. Only Christ's shed blood can make us clean before a holy and righteous God. But once we choose to respond to His loving ransom through His pure and unblemished blood, Paul teaches us to keep our hearts clean. He compares it to the contents of a person's house. "The Lord knows those who are His, and let everyone who names (herself by) the name of the Lord give up all iniquity and stand aloof from it. But in a great house there are not only vessels of gold and silver, but also (utensils) of wood and earthenware, and some for honorable and noble (use) and some for menial and ignoble (use)" (2 Tim. 2:19–20, AMP).

A pearled life values the cleansing offered at the cross. The *crucifixion* (excruciating purging of sin on the cross) provides a clean house. When Christ looks at your heart house, He sees it as clean. But that's not all. Father sent the Holy Spirit to you for ongoing housekeeping. See how Paul teaches us to cooperate with the Holy Spirit in keeping a pure heart: "So whoever cleanses himself (from what is ignoble and unclean, who separates himself from contact with contaminating and corrupting influences) will (then himself) be a vessel set apart and useful for honorable and noble purposes, consecrated and profitable to the Master, fit and ready for any good work. Shun youthful lusts and flee from them, and aim at and pursue righteousness, all that is virtuous and good, right living, conformity to the will of God in thought, word, and deed; (and aim at and pursue) faith, love and peace which is (harmony and concord with others) in fellowship with all (Christians), who call upon the Lord out of a pure heart" (2 Tim. 2:21–22).

Your heart and mine is not pure on its own. Going to church, reading the Bible, doing church activities, and avoiding certain behaviors by themselves will not make you pure. Purity is often thought of as simply an avoidance of certain things or seeking to achieve some level of performance over a list of behaviors. However, a pure heart grows from an increasing awareness of who Christ really is, an increasing love for Him, and the ongoing decision to let Him protect you from what He already cleaned out of your life.

But this is not for a pat on the back. In fact, when purity really begins to grip your heart, you will be so in love with Him that you absolutely detest sin's former grip. You simply become pure because you are one with pure. You are what you bathe in.

Tiny pearls bathe in up to five liters of deep and cleansing saltwater daily, becoming clean, prepared, and ready to reflect glory—of perfect imperfections. Real shimmer.

I will refer back to my story for a moment. The relationship I was in at the time of my surprise pregnancy had been built around activities and attitudes that were not pure. I had become so compartmentalized in my thinking that I didn't even realize how darkened my heart had become. My head told me everything was okay as long as everything looked okay on the outside. My heart told me everything was okay as long as I was happy and everyone approved of and liked me. This created compartments where I would say one thing to please people and environments, but actually behave differently when no one was watching. I struggled to be emotionally honest with myself and others. This is compartmentalizing, and it leads to a place of deep inner conflict because the compartments will run into each other in real life. There is no real peace in a compartmentalized life.

For example, I could attend church during that time and look like a genuine participant. I could sing the songs, know the Bible passages and say the right words. But when I was with my boyfriend, who wasn't into church and God so much, I would do and say things that were different than what I had said in church.

So at the time I found out I was pregnant, he suggested going to see a priest. At that appointment, the priest challenged us on purity and life-giving choices and I was in deep conflict. He and I had not based our relationship on those ideas, and all my looking good on the outside was in the ditch as I sat pregnant in a priest's office with my boyfriend. The inner conflict was so great that I actually had physical reactions to it. I suffered greatly for weeks with heart palpitations, difficulty breathing, and the inability to stop crying. My compartments were in a great battle!

Acting pure on the outside but making dark choices in secrecy is exactly what Jesus came to save us from. His work on the cross enables us to live in peace and agreement between the outside of our life and the inside. Jesus refers to this power-packed principle in Luke 11:34–37: "No one, when he has lit a lamp, puts it in a secret place or under a basket, but on a lampstand, that those who come in may see the light. The lamp of the body is the eye. Therefore, when your eye is good, your whole body also is full of light. But when your eye is bad, your body also is full of darkness. Therefore take heed that the light which is in you is not darkness. If then your whole body is full of light, having no part dark, the whole body will be full of light, as when the bright shining of a lamp gives you light."

As the story continues, a Pharisee ends up inviting Jesus over to his house for a meal. It was customary to wash hands before dinner, and when they noticed Jesus reclining at the table without doing so, they responded to him with astonishment. And here is Jesus's response to them in verse 39: "Now you Pharisees cleanse the outside of the cup and of the plate, but inside you yourselves are full of greed and robbery and extortion and malice and wickedness. You senseless *foolish, stupid* ones *acting without reflection or intelligence*! Did not He who made the outside make the inside also? But *dedicate your inner self and* give as donations to the poor of those things which are within *of inward righteousness* and behold, everything is purified and clean for you" (Luke 11:39–41, AMP).

Before I met the boyfriend I sat with in the priest's office (Sully's father), I had ended an engagement. Impure sexual behavior began during the relationship with my former fiancé. The dark place was kept hidden (though I am sure no one would have cared if I was open about it) from everyone around me. Any light that indwelled me was kept under a bushel, and when I ended that relationship I was poised, due to the former choices, for deepening my impure thoughts, cravings, and choices. I wore a facade to look healthy and pure on the outside, but I was living in the dark secretly. I had developed pride in being able to say I was still a virgin, much like the Pharisee Jesus spoke to who was all about keeping the expectation of washing hands before dinner. I ranked myself amongst the pure because I had not *crossed the line* of impurity. But what I didn't understand about purity was that it begins on the inside, not in a cultural system of religious and moral rules, lines, and appearances. A girl can lose her purity long before she loses her virginity.

Any professor or psychologist at the time would have told me my journey was healthy and normal. But only a God-loving person would have loved me enough to tell me the journey was an impure one. Unfortunately, I didn't have that kind of person in my life at the time, and so I thought I was okay because my life *looked* okay. I had followed the rules. While holding the line, sexual habits, images, and thoughts developed in my relationship with the fiancé that needed to be fed in the next relationship. This led me to a place I never wanted to be.

I became pregnant, unmarried, and not even engaged! In the seventies this was still humiliating and so shameful; and it is this dark shame that motivated many girls, including me, to go to abortion clinics. When the power of shame is greater than the preciousness of a baby, you can bet the darkness has taken over the inner heart.

At such a low point in my life, I was perfectly set up to recognize my true need for real love and relationship with Jesus Christ.

Perfect Work

The Father's heart sent pure love and perfect holiness through Jesus. Think of it like a perfectly written love letter sent from heaven to earth.

> My precious daughter,
>
> I love you deeply and I created you to be mine first. I made you to be a vessel of light—a picture of oneness

with me. You are my beloved. But you put my lamp aside and even hide it at times. How it grieves me. When other things and people are in a higher place of affection, I am jealous. You keep seeking sexual lusts, material wealth, and approval of man, popularity, independence, honor, and recognition ahead of me. I often see that I am the furthest from your mind, and most certainly your heart. It hurts me to see you chasing after so many things, even some good things, only to find yourself hurt, abandoned, and empty over and over. It hurts you. I see the damage it is doing. But I have a way for you to be clean in your mind and motives. I have a way for you to have peace with me, yourself, and others. Just desire me and enter into the brokenness of realizing the darkness of where you have been and how it has hurt you. Grieve for me as I have grieved for you. I will come, I will receive you, and I will lift you from the pit. I long to put my arms around you and clean you up, sweet daughter. Let your desire for me awaken. In your pure sorrow, I will come to you. Love and purity will be in my arms.

You are lovely sweet daughter,

Your Heavenly Father

Five months after I walked into that abortion clinic, Jesus met me in that same bedroom where the conception had occurred. I didn't hear the audible words in the love letter above, but He spoke them to my heart. I was so broken over my life, my confusion, lack of peace and the guilt of abortion that I literally dropped to my knees and wept from a place I didn't even know existed. As the tears flowed down my face onto that bed, I cried out to God and said, "I give up. Please forgive me. I tried to do it right, but I don't feel right inside anymore. If you are real, and you are who you say you are, I am asking you to come into my life. Please remove this darkness I feel, take control of my life, and do with it what you want. I don't care how extreme you get with me, I am just done. I give you my life." Immediately, as if He entered the physical realm and touched my heart and mind, there was a sensation of cleansing that entered my entire body. It felt like he bathed me in fresh water and did so with a smile on His face as if to say, "Welcome home, sweet daughter—let's get you all cleaned up."

From that point on, I never looked back. The purity of that momentous bath motivated me to seek Him with everything I knew, which was very limited at the time.

I can't say that I maintained a pure heart and body at all times for the next six years until I married, but I can say the pattern of purity and desire for it was constantly in play. I still cry when I think about the grace that was covering me during those years. I was able to enter my wedding night hotel room with a pure heart and holding the anticipation of a virgin. God gave me a husband who treated me like a precious daughter of God, who treasured and sought to preserve my restored purity. Only God does that!

What saddens me greatly, as I write this book, is that Christian girls and women don't believe that heart purity or sexual purity is really possible in this day and age. I can spend hours of time in emotional healing, counseling, and prayer with women and hearing all their churchy answers and theological understandings, only to find out days or weeks later, they didn't really believe it is possible to have this profound oneness with pure Christ. Because of the lack of belief, they made decisions as though it wasn't possible. Birth control, sleepovers, and sex with their Christian boyfriend all while they attend church, Bible studies, lead worship, and small groups. Like me, they have compartmentalized their lives and honestly believe they can live every area in the light and keep one in the dark. Because it's just too hard and too high of an expectation. They're right. It is too high of an expectation for the flesh. Jesus's perfect work on the cross, however, provides a way to walk you over the threshold of physical bondage into a relationship whose identity is not based on physical pleasure, but grace, love, purity, and resurrection power.

Ask for Jesus. He will come and purity will be in His arms. Seeking to walk in the flesh by white knuckling it is not a pursuit of purity. White knuckling it is as fleshly as the lusting. The point of purity can be clearly missed. Purity far surpasses cultural and Christian expectations and hoop jumping. It is the by-product of a deep and personal relationship of oneness with Jesus and allowing Him to be the purifier instead of fleshly attempts at rules and rituals.

Virgins can be impure on wedding day.

Jesus is the bridegroom. You are His bride. And He's coming to get you. Do you want to be found in His love, retrieved from your oyster in purity or shame and doubt? Jesus, the perfect human picture of God's heart, was sent to spill out the necessary blood offering. Someone had to pay to ransom purity because it was stolen in the garden. There was no way for man to get it back on his own, but only through the releasing of blood and the satisfaction of wrath. The entire Old Testament, from Genesis 3:7, where Adam and Eve's eyes (the lamp of their body) were opened to their sin, to Jesus's death and resurrection, animal sacrifices had to be made on a regular basis just to get the attention of God. Not one blood sacrifice was ever pure enough to gain the absolute approval of the pure heart of God. No animal or human activity alone could *eternally* satisfy the wrath. In fact, many a high priest was struck dead in the presence of God due to the blood sacrifice's imperfections.

In the Old Testament, certain priests would take an animal and slit its throat to spill blood on the altar. It happened in a place called the Holy of Holies inside the tabernacle. The spilling of blood would *temporarily* satisfy the wrath of God's heart. His holiness absolutely could not coexist with impurity, and it still can't.

God cannot share His inheritance in heaven with impurity, so He sent Jesus who was the blameless One that would open up the access to purity, both for eternity and on earth. This offering serves up forgiveness of sin which results in a clean conscience and life as well as peace for anyone who receives it. Jesus endured the perfect mess, perfect conspiracy, perfect betrayal, and perfect blame that painfully arrived from the spiritual realm to the earth, piercing darkness and impurity as it came. Once this darkness was pierced by spotless blood, the quest for purity was satisfied. Once and for All. Period.

Bathed in Knowledge and Truth

When we receive God's forgiveness, it cleanses our disposition toward sin forever. We are scrubbed clean and cleared for customs at heaven's entrance, once and for all. But even though we are given power to say no to our sinful disposition, we will develop what is called sinful inventory. Purity of heart comes through ongoing awareness of the sins that are stacking up in the present day and the ongoing longing for God's way more than your own way.

A Pearl Girl receives her cleansing through His payment for her. But she will not likely experience a clean conscience and acquire purity if she is not tapping into the knowledge and truth of the cleansing on a daily basis. Joy, a lighter heart, and a clean conscience are continuously established, as we walk in the knowledge and truth of what He did for us.

Hebrews 10:22–23: "Let us draw near with a true heart in full assurance of faith having our hearts sprinkled from an evil conscience and our bodies washed with pure water."

A stronger desire to stay clean and be connected to God, the Great Cleaner, will often follow the initial cleansing. The purification process that God's presence infuses is great gain to a Pearl Girl as her heart purity becomes centered on Him. When she stays on Him, His purity, holiness, grace, and love infuse into her—filling her with light! You can see that this is not performance based, and definitely results in maintained hunger for purity. Encountering a heavenly bath is precious, especially in relationship to the darkness being washed off.

Do you know His gentle and kind hand is leading you to purity? Do you know how much you are valued by this pure and holy God, and that you can continually desire and experience Him? Do you know that He will come with forgiveness and purity in His arms, and a smile on His face? After all, He has known you since before the foundation of the world because you are His idea! Once you know Him and the power of His cleansing, your values change. Earthly pleasures fade in comparison to the pleasure of being treasured and infused with purity.

After I experienced that spiritual bath in my bedroom, cleansed from my sin was no longer a concept from Sunday school and just another sermon. I encountered the great cleanser. That decision and experience was my reference point for the next stage of my Christian life. I could more easily tell when I was getting messy and impure again because I had been cleansed. It's easier to recognize and know when dirt begins to appear again in a house that has been deeply cleansed. A deeply cleansed house requires cleaning daily to maintain its beauty!

I began to catch myself in lustful thoughts before they advanced to the planning stage and acting on them. Reading my Bible gave me truth on what to do instead. God began placing pure-hearted people in my life as I sought purity. One of them directed me to this passage: Philippians 4:8–9: "Brethren, whatever is true, whatever is worthy of reverence and is honorable and seemly, whatever is just, whatever is pure, whatever is lovely and lovable, whatever is kind and winsome and gracious, if there is any virtue and excellence, if there is anything worthy of praise, think on and weigh and take account of these things (fix your minds on them). Practice what you have learned and received and heard and seen in me, and model your way of living on it, and the God of peace (of untroubled, undisturbed well-being) will be with you."

Truth is initiated in the mind. A pure-hearted girl will seek to keep the eye of her mind pure.

Romans 8:6 says, "For to be carnally minded is death, but to be spiritually minded is life and peace."

When God is given permission, His kind Spirit pierces your heart to show you your personal sin and leads you to repent, to come clean. In that moment, you are spiritually minded. Capture it! House it! The result of repentance is always peace. Tasting true peace gives a pearl girl an appetite for more peace, and so she begins to value that more than the fun of her sin. This is the beginning of knowledge.

purified in the battle, and equipped. His presence helps me recognize the enemy's lies and strategy that may be trying to trap me in an offense. (Ps. 23:4–6, Rev. 15:3)

His perfect love casts out fear. When I am afraid of outcomes and powerlessness, I have a Savior who always moves and acts in my best interest. No matter the face of fear, the power of His love is greater. Knowing Him gives me the authority to send fear away. (2 Tim. 1:7, Ps. 112:7–8, John 4:18)

There is no shame and condemnation. Father can enjoy looking at me because the wrath has already been satisfied. I experience smiling and singing over my life. I may grieve our love relationship at times, but this grief serves to help me return in godly sorrow and repentance. When my heart learns to break for the same things His heart breaks for, I will enjoy sitting at His banqueting table. (Zeph. 3:17; Rom. 8:1)

His power can conquer and subdue, so I will call on Him and intimately pound heaven until He does.

Guarding your heart in Christ Jesus is believing all these truths about God and yourself and refusing any lies that the enemy wants to whisper to you about your situation. Guarding your heart in these truths will nurture purity in your heart and life. But there is nothing more upside down than believing and following a set of rules will make you pure.

Tiny pearls bathe in up to five liters of deep and cleansing saltwater daily. Becoming clean, prepared, and ready to reflect glory—of perfect imperfections. Real shimmer.

Do you bathe in the endless supply of His love and presence for daily cleansing? Are you being prepared and ready to reflect His image? Imago Dei. Glory.

Oh what a shimmering beauty you are! Can you see the delight in His smile? I can't stop smiling as I write this.

My dear daughter,

You are becoming a pearl. But you must seek my heart to find fulfillment for your deepest longings. Everything beautiful in your life is directly from me or a reflection of how I feel about you. You had a darkened mind and many heart impurities before you began to seek me wholeheartedly. Do not let pride and lies become stronger in you than my love.

I am your love shelter. I had the idea of you before the foundations of the world and I took delight in it. Like the pearl forming inside the oyster host, I planted you in your mother's womb, an imperfect host, and carried you through to this very day. I knew you would have difficulties, but I have waited for you to turn toward me and see that I am passionate about you and have a purpose for your presence. You are meant to be. I love you.

Come home. Live and move and have your being from here.

Your heavenly Father

Conclusion

THE BEAUTIFUL JAPANESE pearl divers historically known as Ama would dive deep ocean waters to develop and harvest pearls. They would dive nude. Their bodies, which housed more fat cells than men, would serve them well as they would free dive to incredible depths, either to plant pearl or retrieve them. The finest pearls come from deep, clear, and rapid waters. Ama would brave many dangerous elements such as sharks, poisonous jellyfishes, dangerous water depths, frigid waters, and body decompressions in order to retrieve the treasured pearls.

Jesus, your bridegroom, experienced the ultimate depth through pain and submission. He hung nude on a cross, braved religious flesh-eating sharks (the poison and toxins of your sin), and the frigidity of His own Father turning His face from His son. His body decompressed into a sacred separation from His Father so you could be found, loved, and known.

Father sent Jesus into the depths to retrieve you, call you by name, and purchase you. You are His and He is yours.

> You are found.
> You are reclaimed from the depths.
> You are loved.
> Know and be known all the days of your life.

Afterword

DURING THE WRITING of this book, my birth mother passed away. I raced across the country in a series of flights to experience a loving good-bye between us. But when I arrived, just like that empty bedroom fifty-three years ago, she was *gone* before I got there. At first, that feeling of abandonment met me with "she left already…again." But the affection of Father nudged me and pointed to the pearls I had been gathering through the years. Everywhere His hand had touched that wound through the years, He had left a pearl in its place. I was *loved, reclaimed,* and found true and lasting *affection.* I had received and offered forgiveness to *endure* the pain, and He had *purified* me throughout the process.

So I stood beside my imperfect host, my mother's lifeless body, and said good-bye to her and shouted in gratitude at the same time, "I am not abandoned! You are here, Jesus, just like you always were."

As I prepared for her memorial service, I sought to find photos of mother and I, and much to my disappointment, there were none. But God did show me a different photograph.

This photo *shown here* was taken when my adoptive parents were newlyweds, and I was two years old. There I was, still under the care of my birth mom, but in a photo between my *future* parents who were, at the time, my aunt and uncle. I heard Father's kind voice say to me as I held that photo and wept, "I put you in your momma's womb to be *their* child. You are meant to be."

> Abandoned to Loved.
> Betrayal to Beauty.
> Parasite to Pearl.

Pearl Couture

Principles and Biblical Truths

"EVERY GIRL OR woman must be so hidden in Christ that (a) man must go through God to get to her" (2 Peter 3:1–5).

To experience lasting relationships, we must form new filters for living and relating and decision-making. Insecurities only serve to be bait for Satan to use against us and all our relationships.

Purity of Heart

"I am created and valued by a pure and holy God and this value changes what I value."

Purity of heart is based on God's holiness, grace, and love. It is not performance based and results in a desire for living a pure life.

Endurance for the Battle

"I can endure anything this life brings my way through knowing the value and love of this pure and holy God. I can love, respect, and forgive myself and others. I know what a girl must wear to endure the spiritual battle."

Endurance is required for a lifelong race in a young girl's Christian life. Living the Christian life in today's American culture is not for the fainthearted.

Affections

"Regarding God in Christ Jesus as my highest affection in devotion and decisions will open His heart intimately to me where He will show me my daily path."

Longing, delight, humility, submission, and trust will serve to keep me in a close and intimate connection with Jesus Christ above all other affections and bonds.

Reclaim

"I will reclaim what is rightfully mine in Christ Jesus and refuse to fall for the enemy's every day attempts to break me down. I will seek to position myself in the confidence of Christ's perfect work in all attacks against my girlhood and future womanhood."

Reclaim any godly inheritance the enemy has stolen through lies I have believed and acted on concerning myself and others.

Love

"He takes delight in me, saw fit for me to be born, and has a purpose and passion for my existence. I will be found, held together, and grown up in the love of Jesus Christ. All feelings of earthly love will first be subject to God's unconditional and eternal love."

Love never fails. Love is a knowledge; a place where I am known and secured. It is not a feeling and cannot be found in human effort.

PEARLHOOD ©

The development of a girl's wholeness in her inner core (her sense of value and identity) involves all 5 of these areas. Lack of development in any one layer will create a weak area inviting lies and destructive behavior to enter, risking deterioration of all parts. Each area is a part of the whole.

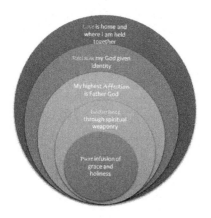

Love is home and where I am held together

Reclaim my God given identity

My highest Affection is Father God

Endure lives through spiritual weaponry

Pure infusion of grace and holiness